Out of the Ashes

Burned Churches
and the Community of Faith

EDITED BY
NORMAN A. HJELM

THOMAS NELSON PUBLISHERS
Nashville

In Memoriam

THE REVEREND DR. MAC CHARLES JONES

1950–1997

"His awareness of the meaning of the burned churches and his ministry on their behalf will remain as a hallmark of his service."

Printed in the United States of America
1 2 3 4 5 6 — 02 01 00 99 98 97

Contents

Burned Churches Timeline

Jan 13—Macedonia Missionary Baptist Church in Bales, TN, was burned.

1995

Mar 14—New Outreach Community Center in Charlotte, NC, was destroyed.

May 7—Faith Christian Family Center in Tallahassee, FL, was burned.

Jun 3—Salem AME Church in Greensboro, FL, was burned. Greater Mt. Zion Tabernacle Church of God in Christ, Portsmouth, VA, was burned.

Nov 18—St. Mark's Missionary Baptist Church in Tyronza, AR, was destroyed.

Dec 30—Salem Baptist Church, Fruitland, TN, was burned.

Jan 8—Inner City Church in Knoxville, TN, was firebombed.

1996

Feb 28—New Liberty Baptist Church, Tyler, AL, was burned.

Apr 16—Fire at the First Baptist Church in Richmond, VA.

Apr 18—NCCC member heads pledged their support for an investigation of the burnings.

May 21—Dr. Mac Charles Jones testified on the burnings before the House Judiciary Committee.

May 22—NCCC called the burnings a national disaster and a national disgrace.

Jun 6—Matthews Murkland Presbyterian Church, Charlotte, NC, destroyed by arson.

Jun 8—NCCC encouraged President Clinton to form the National Church Arson Task Force.

Jun 9–10—NCCC flew 38 pastors, whose churches were vandalized, for conferences with President Clinton, Attorney General Reno, Secretary Robert Rubin and members of Congress.

Jun 11—NCCC launched the Burned Churches Fund. The Ford Foundation with seven other major foundations pledged $2.7 million to the fund.

Jun 12—Dr. Campbell and Dr. Jones represented the NCCC at an interfaith "Ecumenical Service" in South Carolina; President Clinton spoke.

Jun 17—Central Grove Missionary Baptist Church in Kossuth, MS, was destroyed. Mt. Pleasant Missionary Baptist Church burned in Kossuth, MS.

Jun 20—Dr. Jones testified before the Congressional Black Caucus.

Jun 26—Pastors from burned churches, accompanied by General Secretary Campbell, joined Clinton for breakfast at the White House.

Jun 27—God's Chapel in Athens, TN, was burned due to racial motivation.

Jun 18–26—Congress unanimously passes the Arson Prevention Act of 1996.

Jun 28–30—South Carolina Christian Action Council hosted a "Sabbath of Support."

July—NCCC contracted Habitat for Humanity to join the rebuilding effort.

Jul 3—President Clinton signs the Arson Prevention Act of 1996 into law.

Jul 15—3,000 people assembled at the historic Abyssinian Baptist Church in Harlem, NY, for support of burned churches.

1996

Aug 6—Pamela McDonald of the Fine Arts Museum of San Francisco, CA, presented $20,000 to the Burned Churches Fund. Central Grove Missionary Baptist Church, Kossuth, MS, received a modest emergency grant from the Burned Churches Fund.

Aug 11—Groundbreaking ceremonies at St. Paul's Primitive Baptist Church, Lauderdale, MS.

Aug 12—"The Churches Are Burning," a program about the current epidemic of hate-motivated attacks on Afro-American churches, aired on the Faith & Values Cable Channel; repeat airing on Sep 23.

Aug 15—NCCC has received $5 million in cash, pledges and in-kind contributions to the Burned Churches Fund to date.

Aug 19—NCCC led an interfaith delegation to the reconstruction site of Salem Baptist Church, Fruitland, TN; the Clintons and the Gores participated.

Aug 28—"New York Undercover" donated $13,000 to the Burned Churches Project and featured a two-part episode on church burnings in Harlem.

Sep 7—A National Church Rebuilding Initiative was launched co-chaired by HUD, NCCC and the Congress of National Black Churches (CNBC) in Memphis, TN.

Sep 26–29—Church Rebuilding Project Conference held in Birmingham, AL.

Sep 27—U.S. Olympic Basketball's Dream Team donated subsidy of $150,000 given by Olympic Committee.

Oct 12—Fourth meeting of the rebuilding initiative in New Orleans, LA.

Oct 16—To date, more than $7 million in cash, pledges and in-kind contributions of goods and services have been received by the Burned Churches Fund.

Oct 18—Burned Churches Fund received a grant of $250,000 from the Robert Wood Johnson Foundation.

Oct 24–26—Emergency Conference on Racism sponsored by the NCCC was held in Columbia, SC.

1997

Feb 15—The first team of college students was brought in to help rebuild burned churches— "Spring Rebuild."

Feb–Mar—Seven more African-American churches burned.

Mar 6—The Rev. Dr. Mac Charles Jones died of an embolism (blood clot).

Mar 12—Memorial services for the Rev. Dr. Mac Charles Jones.

Mar 16–26—St. Mark's Missionary Baptist Church in AR rebuilt in 10-day blitz.

Apr 11–12—Unveiling of the monument to the burned churches on Allen University's campus in Columbia, South Carolina; the unveiling was followed by a march against hatred and racism from the campus to the State House.

TO DATE . . .

More than $25 million in local contributions, grants from the burned Churches Fund, in-kind gifts, HUD guaranteed loans and insurance payments have been allocated to address the burned churches epidemic.

Preface

Throughout its history as a vital force for salvation and change in the world, the Church of Jesus Christ has consistently made its most valiant witness in the midst of chaotic and traumatic situations and times. That was certainly a reality in the experience of the National Council of the Churches of Christ in the United States of America (NCCC) as we became involved in what has come to be known as the "burned churches" crisis.

In 1995 there were spasmodic reports of African American churches being burned in various communities, mostly in the South. Casual contacts began to reveal a pattern that was cause for concern. A closer look, by contacting pastors and people in those burned churches, revealed that the people were living under terror and fear, and civil and law enforcement authorities were suspected of not naming the reality of what was happening. The NCCC responded by expressing solidarity with the victims and facilitated the process whereby they could share their experiences with the appropriate authorities and seek redress for their concerns.

Though law enforcement and justice authorities were initially slow in responding, they eventually joined the churches in a more aggressive investigation. It was revealed that most of the burnings resulted from acts of racial hate and violence by persons related to various known hate groups. Thus it was that the NCCC with its member churches placed the national spotlight on the burned churches, which resulted in it being called a national disaster.

When the NCCC sent out the call for the churches and the peoples of the nation to respond to this crisis, we were overwhelmed at the spirit of generosity and good will exhibited by churches, businesses, corporations, and the people in general. When people are mistreated by acts of hate and violence, people of good will never cease to respond in various ways.

As I reflect on what happened through the Burned Churches Fund, it is evident to me that the spirit of ecumenism and interfaith witness has here been at its best. The ecumenical and interfaith movement is alive and well at the level where it makes a difference—the hearts and lives of people. Thus, it is appropriate that we now pause and reflect on the theological and ecclesial significance of how persons of faith responded to the call to rebuild these churches that were destroyed by fire. You will find such reflection in the chapters which follow. I am most grateful to all who contributed to the process which made this volume possible.

West Sacramento, California   ***Melvin G. Talbert,*** Bishop
September 1997   The United Methodist Church
                                                      San Francisco Area, and
                                                      President, NCCC, 1996–97

Foreword

Out of the despicable evil of hate attacks on churches and the burning of church buildings, we have witnessed the rebirth of faith and new courage for our life together. It has been a story of hatred overcome. To reflect on the tragic events of this epidemic of burnings is to confront again the mystery of God's Spirit at work in our midst. God has again brought good out of evil, life out of the ashes of death. The central Christian paradigm of the suffering of crucifixion opening the door to the miracle of resurrection has been reenacted.

My witness to what we have experienced together as an ecumenical Christian community in company with our partners of other faith traditions is simply this: my faith has been deepened and my life encouraged. My conviction is that these essays, born out of the rash of the destructive attacks on churches, invites us all into the inner meaning of what has occurred, beyond news reports and headlines.

The National Council of the Churches of Christ in the U.S.A., on behalf of its 33 member national church bodies and millions of American church members in their congregations, became the anchor and manager for a massive response to what was broadly acknowledged as a national horror. No one wants to live in a nation where houses of worship are attacked and burned! This has given me a place at the center of the response. Let me share what I have seen.

As you are well aware, the vast majority of the congregations attacked are congregations of black American Christians. These attacks, confirmed again and again to be rooted in the tenacious racism that plagues the life of our nation and is repeatedly experienced in the communities where we live, have sharpened my awareness of racial hatred and abuse. If there was doubt about such acts of hatred and fear being sins against God, I have seen evidence that erases all doubt forever.

I have seen the deep, determined, courageous, and astonishingly forgiving Christian faith nourished through the African American church tradition. It is wonderfully alive and victorious. The story of the burned churches is finally the story of such faith. Trace it again in the voices of pastors and the insights of leaders and Christian thinkers. Through such faith God has blessed and enlarged my own faith and love.

The response to these tragic events has been overwhelming and encouraging. Almost spontaneous, certainly unplanned or organized, it has come from every sector of the Christian community, from communities of every faith, and from individuals of moral discernment and active good will who may not be participants in any faith community. Hundreds of thousands of people have actively responded through contributing funds, volunteering, reaching out to build healthier communities, and voicing a clear condemnation of racism. In an age of too much disillusionment and cynicism, we cannot fail to consider the deeper currents in our life, religiously fed, that can be claimed and channeled in the service of greater justice and healing.

I have been in a position to see and also to participate in a converging of strengths that has been both remarkable and effective. Barriers of suspicion and distrust, even within the Christian community, have been transcended through what we have done together. The philanthropic community, historically rooted in religious commitments but in recent years estranged from its roots and its heritage partners, discovered a viable means to support and encourage the ecumenical response. Businesses, large and small, again and again found a way to help. The leaders of government—I think of the call of the President and the unanimous and swift enactment of restoration legislation by Congress—became actively engaged in addressing what was soon understood to be an intolerable national disaster.

There is no way such experiences can be allowed to pass into the archives without our thoughtful assessment and our receiving their instructive nourishment. What made us respond almost without hesitation? Why were old antagonisms laid to rest? Can our religious community rediscover its God-given unity? How will the ethical maturities and energies we have seen expressed continue to be developed and nourished? Is religious vitality more truly at the core of our life together than we may have realized?

The struggle with racist hatred and deeply corrosive fear continues. What was accomplished during the years of the civil rights movement insists on being reclaimed and extended. Religious commitment must advocate a fair, open, and opportunity-filled America where all people can embrace the life God intends and thereby come to embrace one another in dignity and neighborliness. Our work together, reinforced by our shared response to the burnings, must move ahead in challenging racism.

Detractors have either decried or defamed the National Council's Burned Churches Project; yet during this last year nearly 100 churches have either been rebuilt or are currently under construction. This gives the lie to such accusations and claims. Now, those same detractors want to confine the tragic events to a moment in history that has now passed or to a social aberration to be noted but then left behind. Men and women of faith know better! These pages invite us to understand the deeper meaning of what has occurred and to "gird up our loins" to overcome evil with good and to seek liberty and justice for all.

My most earnest word to you as you enter the pages of this slim volume is this: we have seen and been participants in the mystery of God's work among us. We cannot fail to be nourished and empowered for continuing faithfulness and unity out of what we have seen, heard, and known. Welcome anew to a partnership in faith and a journey with God!

New York City
October 1997

Joan Brown Campbell
General Secretary
National Council of the Churches
of Christ in the U.S.A.

Introduction

Norman A. Hjelm

In 1963 James Baldwin, whose insights concerning the issue of racism in American life were perhaps unparalleled, published *The Fire Next Time*. Even the title of Baldwin's classic has proven to be prophetic; in several of the essays of the present volume reference is made to the fire this time. And of course the point of reference here is the epidemic of burned African American churches which has occurred in this country in the past few years. "The fire this time," the arson of black houses of worship, is flaming evidence that the virulence of racism continues to burn in our land.

Out of the Ashes: Burned Churches and the Community of Faith is a collection of original essays designed to do several things. Two essays, one by Albert Pennybacker and Donald Rojas and the other by Herb Boyd, tell the stories of the burnings and of the response to this plague by the National Council of the Churches of Christ in the USA through its Burned Churches Project. Movingly, the second of these chapters is largely the actual story of three instances of burned churches as told by the pastors involved. The two following essays, by McKinley Young and Jesse Jackson, Sr., discuss the meaning of these stories from the perspectives of African American church bodies and the African American community at large.

The six subsequent contributions to this book are written by representative theologians from a number of different church traditions: Philip Turner, an Episcopalian; Emmanuel Clapsis, an Orthodox; James Evans, an American Baptist; Deborah Mullen, a Presbyterian; Susan Davies from the United Church of Christ; and William Rusch, a Lutheran. Their concern is to reflect theologically and biblically on issues raised both by racism in American life, a racism also to be found within American churches, and by the ecclesiological and ecumenical significance of the response of Christian churches to the needs of sisters and brothers in the faith. Racism, in these essays, is seen as a sin which contradicts God's will for the unity of the whole human community and also divides the church which is the body of Christ. The response of American churches, together with other communities and persons of good will, to the burned churches is seen as *an ecclesial event,* that is, as the sort of act which is integral to the very being of the church itself as *koinonia,* "the community of faith." These essays, of course, raise a host of other crucial questions concerning the political, social, and moral dimensions of oppressive racism in "the American way of life." The fact that the authors of these essays come from a variety of church backgrounds indicates that several different approaches, sometimes not totally in agreement with one another, are taken toward the issues of the book. The largest portion of this book, then, is a theological and ecclesiological conversation about racism in American life and the relations between communities of faith, relations of *communio* or *koinonia,* as they respond to this particular crisis of racial hate and violence which so seriously threatens African American churches.

Two additional points need to be made concerning the substance and the intention of the book. In the first place, it is important to acknowledge from the beginning that these essays face head on several critical issues which have been raised in connection with the burning of African American churches and with the response of the National Council of Churches to those burnings. Has a *racial conspiracy* really been involved? Indeed, has there been any organized conspiracy at all behind these burnings? If not, is it still correct to speak in terms which echo the comment that "the conspiracy is racism itself"? What, further, is the proper and responsible role of churches in respect to public advocacy, in this case both education and the support of concrete political action concerning the many very specific dimensions of racism in our nation? On just such points as these the National Council of Churches has frequently throughout its history been the object of sharp questioning and criticism and at a number of points in *Out of the Ashes* these criticisms are faced openly and convincingly.

And in the second place, *Out of the Ashes* stands as an attempt from within the life of the NCCC and its many member churches to pursue theological and ecclesiological reflection concerning the actions and programs carried out by the Council and those churches. Ecumenism in America has often been charged by its critics, incorrectly and frequently with hostility, as consisting almost exclusively in non-reflective programs of "liberal social action." The fact is, however, that serious and rigorous theological reflection does take place within the ecumenical movement, and this volume is a public demonstration of that fact. It is, moreover, perhaps most often the Commission on Faith and Order of the NCCC which is the locus of this kind of thoughtful reflection. Faith and Order is that entity, of church leaders and scholars, charged with working theologically to discover and recover dimensions of the visible unity of the church, including not only matters of doctrine, sacramental worship, and polity, but also difficult and sometimes contentious and church-dividing ethical issues which contribute to the shaping of Christian witness in the world. It is Faith and Order which first suggested the preparation of this volume and in all of its variety and even weakness the book is to be seen as its contribution to furthering the unity which God, in Christ and through the Holy Spirit, wills for the church, its mission, and the entire creation. Ecumenism is about just such unity.

The editor of *Out of the Ashes* is grateful to hosts of colleagues: to those who, sometime amidst extremely busy schedules, have contributed to the volume, offering their experience and their insight; and to the staff at Thomas Nelson Publishers who under the considerable pressures of a virtually impossible schedule have bent every effort to make this publication timely and widely distributed. The President and General Secretary of the National Council of the Churches of Christ in the USA, Melvin Talbert and Joan Brown Campbell, have been unstinting in their encouragement and support of the project. And three NCCC staff persons have worked tirelessly on behalf of this publication: Albert Pennybacker through whose office the Burned Churches Project has taken place; Donald Rojas who as Director of that project has made an enduring contribution to the healing of this nation in a time of serious crisis; and William Rusch who originally conceived of this book as, in the widest sense, a contribution of Faith and Order to increased understanding in our society and unity within the church of Jesus Christ.

It is fitting that *Out of the Ashes* be dedicated to the memory of the Rev. Dr. Mac Charles Jones whose untimely death occurred on March 6, 1997. Dr. Jones, who had shortly before his death joined the staff of the National Council of Churches as Associate General Secretary for National Ministries, was perhaps that person who more than any other in our community understood racism in nation and church, who lifted his voice loudly in active concern for those among us who are the most oppressed, and who inspired and led the Council and its member churches through the Burned Churches Project to act swiftly and healingly for the extinction of the fire this time.

1

A Time to Heal: The Burned Churches Project

Albert Pennybacker and Donald Rojas

A Quiet Epidemic

Racially motivated church burnings are not a new phenomenon in the United States. There have been several periods in the nation's history—the first just after the Civil War—when the burning and bombing of black churches occurred at alarming rates. While the current period of burnings appears to have started in the 1980s, it intensified in 1995. Fifty black churches were known to have been victims of arson from 1990 to 1995. By 1996 and early 1997, that number had quadrupled.

The National Council of the Churches of Christ in the USA (NCCC) became aware of this dramatic increase in racially motivated burnings, largely on the basis of investigations carried out by the Center for Democratic Renewal (CDR) in Atlanta, an organization founded in 1979 as the National Anti-Klan Network. Those investigations revealed that a catastrophe of enormous national proportions was taking shape—a quiet epidemic of racial violence was clearly again working its way across the country.

More than church buildings were going up in flames. Black churches are the centers of their communities. Weddings, funerals, parties, meetings, schooling—most aspects of social life—revolve around the black church. The burnings that took place between 1990 and 1997 were both violent and tragically destructive. Those who set the fires clearly intended the damage to be swift and complete, and their message to be loud and clear. Hate graffiti, such as "kill the niggers," "white is right," and the drawing of a noose around the word "nigger," were found on smoky walls still standing in the rubble. Fire accelerants diminished many churches to nothing more than ashes. Death threats were made to pastors and laity. The fires claimed at least one human life, Peter Adams, a 23-year-old black man, a member of the fire-destroyed South Richland Bibleway Church in Richland County, South Carolina.

"We've got to act."

The number of fires rose dramatically in early 1995. In January of that year alone, seven churches were burned. Alarmed, the NCCC, America's oldest and largest national ecumenical organization, began to organize. Its General Secretary, the Rev. Dr. Joan Brown Campbell, insisted, "These are our churches. We've got to act."

Prior to the burnings, the NCCC, comprised of 33 national Protestant and Orthodox church bodies, had declared racial justice its first priority and named Mac Charles Jones, pastor of St. Stephen's Baptist Church in Kansas City, Missouri, the General Secretary's Associate for Racial Justice. In cooperation with the CDR and the Center for Constitutional Rights (CCR), the NCCC sent teams of concerned persons to visit with the pastors of the burned churches and their communities. The response to the crisis was swift. Dr. Jones urged the leadership of the NCCC to awaken the nation to what was clearly an expanding national and human tragedy. United Methodist Bishop Melvin G. Talbert, then serving as President of the NCCC, led the Council's highest deliberative body to commit staff and resources to respond both pastorally and prophetically. The Burned Churches Project was born. In May of 1996 the NCCC executive board declared the attacks on black churches a "national disaster" and established the Burned Churches Fund. The NCCC set a goal of $1 million from the disaster funds of its 33-member communions to help rebuild the burned churches, then numbered at 46.

The NCCC leadership also urged President Clinton to speak out on this issue. On June 8, 1996 the President gave his weekly radio address to the nation with ministers from burned and vandalized churches standing at his side. They were part of a 38-member contingent brought to Washington by the NCCC to discuss the situation with President Clinton, Attorney General Janet Reno, Treasury Secretary Robert Rubin, and members of Congress. While in Washington, the NCCC helped to focus political and media attention on the rash of church burnings. Little media attention had up to that point been directed to this problem, with the notable exception of the remarks at halftime of a January 8 National Football League game by Reggie White, star of the Green Bay Packers and himself the pastor of an African American Baptist church in Tennessee. In point of fact it was White who gave the burned churches crisis its first national exposure.

The very weekend of the first NCCC-led delegation to Washington, five more churches were burned or vandalized in Texas, Georgia, and South Carolina. That Monday, the front page of *The New York Times* pictured the burning of Matthews Murkland Presbyterian Church, a North Carolina church of historic importance within the African American community. Within days of the *Times* article, the NCCC held a news conference in Washington dealing with its investigative findings concerning the burned churches. President Clinton also then established the National Church Arson Task Force to coordinate efforts of the Federal Bureau of Investigation (FBI) and the Bureau of Alcohol, Tobacco, and Firearms (BATF) in dealing with the crisis. Attorney General Reno tripled the number of agents deployed to work with local and state law enforcement agencies, churches, and concerned citizens' groups. At this time Congress also acted by voting unanimously to stiffen penalties for church-related arson, increasing the maximum sentence to 20 years imprisonment. Further, it committed $10 million in bank loan guarantees to the rebuilding effort and authorized more than $12 million to support the BATF's role in the national task force.

Word soon came that the initial number of churches burned due to racial hatred, bigotry, and violence had grown from 46 to 70. Within a year that number grew to 124. The NCCC's goal was quickly raised to $2 million, and then to $12 million in applicable resources.

A Wider Partnership

Support was strong from nongovernmental sources as well. The Ford Foundation gave courageous leadership in approaching a number of philanthropic foundations for contributions. These included the Annenberg, W. K. Kellogg, John D. & Catherine T.

MacArthur, Charles S. Mott, and Rockefeller Foundations and the Pew Charitable Trusts. The Ford Foundation urged them to join both to reconstruct the burned churches and to fight against this racial and ethnic hatred. One foundation participant remarked, "We must make it clear that there is no place for this behavior in our democratic society."

Together, these foundations pledged $2.7 million to the NCCC's Burned Churches Fund. Others responded with gifts, including a contribution of $250,000 from the Robert Wood Johnson Foundation. The Burned Churches Fund thus became the single largest funding resource for the rebuilding of the churches and for the necessary antiracism effort.

Further, an unprecedented number of religious organizations of all faiths joined to form an ecumenical and interfaith partnership with the NCCC to "restore the damaged churches and to challenge racism throughout the country." In addition to the 33-member communions of the National Council of Churches, the following became partners in this effort: the American Jewish Committee, the Congress of National Black Churches, the Islamic Circle of North America, the National Conference of Catholic Bishops, the Religious Action Center of Reform Judaism—the Union of American Hebrew Congregations, the Standing Conference of Orthodox Bishops of America, and the Unitarian Universalist Association.

As contributions and communications of support poured in from around the world, the NCCC found itself immersed in an enormous undertaking. It had responsibility for administering the funds and directing a significant rebuilding effort. The NCCC's goal was to provide up to $100,000 in grant money to each church that needed rebuilding. Its investigations, however, revealed that the average cost per church would be $150,000.

The NCCC released members of its existing staff from normal responsibilities and hired additional temporary staff in order to form an administration to oversee all aspects of the project. The Burned Churches Project office was established and the NCCC also organized a committee, which included Roman Catholic and Jewish religious leaders, civil rights leaders, and others, to oversee the grant-making process. Soon after the committee and administrative team were in place, the NCCC joined forces with the U.S. Department of Housing and Urban Development and the Congress of National Black Churches to establish the National Church Rebuilding Initiative. This partnership became responsible for coordinating the federal loan guarantees and the contributions of labor and materials needed for rebuilding the churches.

Troubling Investigations

One of the most urgent questions which the National Council of Churches and others responding to the burning of churches faced was whether or not these fires were in fact racially motivated. People had been burning churches for centuries and, in recent years, a fair number of church burnings could be traced to insurance fraud or even inner-parish conflicts. What was the actual relation of these burnings to virulent racism?

Investigators of the events of the past few years have discovered that while the rate of arson at nonblack churches has remained steady in recent times, the rate of arson at black churches has skyrocketed. Although black churches comprise only ten percent of churches in the United States, they account for more than fifty percent of the arson fires set. According to these investigations, there is clear evidence of racism directed toward many of the churches. A frightening level of violence has also been uncovered. Fires have been started with the intent to destroy completely. Older churches and many national landmarks have been burned for the second or third time in their history.

What was just as troubling to church leaders was the manner in which the fires were being investigated by law-enforcement officials. Several pastors reported that the victims of the fires were being treated as suspects. A pattern of local officials harassing pastors and church members has been uncovered. Church and personal records of both clergy and laity have been subpoenaed and persons have been subjected to intense questioning and in some cases even to lie-detector tests.

The impact of these church fires has been enormous in ways both tangible and intangible. In a report to President Clinton, the NCCC investigators concluded that more than 20,000 people have been personally affected by the burnings. The cost to rebuild, based on on-site conferences and assessments, clearly requires major resources. The NCCC developed, with the CDR as a consultant to identify racially motivated burnings, an assessment team to determine grant eligibility for the churches. Perhaps the saddest finding of all was that valuable repositories of family history and African American culture have been lost forever to the flames.

Was an organized conspiracy underway? That question has been posed and debated, especially in the investigative media. While causes other than racism have been identified, it is clear that the majority of the attacks on black churches arose from hatred. At least thirteen of the attacks since January 1990 have taken place around the Martin Luther King, Jr. holiday. In addition to evidence of tactics typically used by white supremacist groups, several of those charged with setting the fires have testified about their own racist motivation and their affiliation with the Ku Klux Klan, the Aryan Faction, or other hate groups. The CDR has reported "a disturbing picture of events, connections, activities and supporters of a deeply ingrained set of beliefs."

Noted African American author Anthony Walton has written:

> If, perhaps, there was too great a rush to infer the existence of a nationwide racist conspiracy to terrorize blacks, the great rush to discredit this theory is doubly disturbing. What is disappointing and even maddening about the attitudes of the critics [is] . . . they don't seem to want to acknowledge the psychic trauma and absolute terror that the imagery of burning churches can call up in the minds of African-Americans. It does not matter, in the end, whether the Ku Klux Klan is meticulously plotting the terror in a war room somewhere, because that is its effect. It does not matter whether the fires are being set in an organized conspiracy, by "troubled teens" or a bunch of copycat racists. The churches are being singled out as black institutions, and from the early 1800s onward, it has been common knowledge that churches are the heart—socially, economically and politically . . . That act of violence against a place of such deep resonance is trouble for everyone.

Speaking to a group of Southern governors and senators, President Clinton has said, "As Americans, we consistently and passionately come together to say this crosses racial lines, this crosses party lines and this crosses religious lines. The first freedom in the Constitution, the First Amendment—it enshrines the freedom of religion in America. And whether they are black churches, or white churches, or synagogues or mosques that were burned . . . we cannot tolerate any of it."

Helping Congregations Heal

Money alone cannot rebuild a church. Thousands of people have donated their time and their skills to rebuild church structures. The NCCC retained Habitat for Humanity International to create the Church Rebuilding Project office in Murfreesboro, Tennessee, to coordinate volunteers from all over the country, and to organize work camps to erect new churches.

In the spring of 1997, this Church Rebuilding Project and Christmas in April*USA worked together to create "Spring Rebuild." This program brought together more than 60 groups of high school and college students, over 1000 individuals, to four work camps in Florida, Virginia, and Tennessee. One organizer remarked, "This is an opportunity to help people who have been touched by the pain of those who lost their churches to arson. We hope this will help congregations heal."

Keeping Fuel from the Fire

The mission of the Burned Churches Project has gone beyond simply providing the bricks, mortar, and volunteers to erect new structures. The healing process includes addressing the hatred behind these racist attacks. More than just rebuilding, it has been important to restore a sense of community and build networks of support to help prevent such violence from happening again.

This mission has been implemented in many ways. Before churches are rebuilt, those involved assess the risks these churches face. Fire-retardant materials, fire alarms, and exterior lighting are essential for protecting the churches in the future. The Burned Churches Project helped some churches in remote, isolated areas purchase land closer to town for rebuilding their churches. Some communities initiated security patrols to decrease the risk of future damage. Funding has also helped secure adequate insurance policies.

Together with these security precautions, the Burned Churches Project is answering a need from pastors and congregations to help them establish a network of support within local communities. These efforts include interfaith and community dialogues on racism, educational activities, and guest preaching programs between different churches. "We're trying to make sure that there is no next time," said one staffer. "But if vandalism strikes again, the pastors can turn to a support network in their own communities. No one should have to struggle with such a challenge alone." Addressing racism is an important part of rebuilding communities and preventing future destruction. "Nobody wants to see these new church buildings merely become the fuel for tomorrow's fires," said another NCCC staff person. "We're taking every step we can to help rebuild the churches wisely and strengthen their place in a caring community."

More Than Bricks and Mortar

The Burned Churches Project has identified 124 churches for rebuilding during the first phase of its program. To date, investigators have identified 65 additional churches that need help and have placed them on a list for Phase Two of the program.

During the Program's first phase, the Burned Churches Project raised more than $7 million in cash and more than $3 million in in-kind material gifts, as well as gifts of voluntary labor put toward this effort. By April 30, 1997, the Burned Churches Project Grant Committee had awarded more than $4.5 million in cash grants. By the same time, the rebuilding of 25 churches had been overseen and 60 more churches were under construction. During the summer of 1997 it was anticipated that ground would be broken for 12 more new churches. By January 1997, technical teams had visited 90 churches to assess their particular financial circumstances and reconstruction plans, as well as to determine whether the grants already given were adequate to permit satisfactory rebuilding.

As the Burned Churches Project goes forward into new phases it is intended that greater emphasis will be put on rebuilding communities and on program initiatives that affirm and embody Martin Luther King, Jr.'s vision of "the beloved community." Dr. King once said, when speaking of fellow Americans who stood by him in the civil rights struggle, "Their destiny is tied up with our destiny, and they have come to realize that their freedom is inextricably bound to our freedom. We cannot walk alone."

People who have lost their churches have not had to walk alone. This is the testimony of the Burned Churches Project of the National Council of the Churches of Christ in the USA. Help in constructing new buildings has come from places far beyond anyone's expectations. But rebuilding is about more than just bricks and mortar or stacks of lumber. It is about rebuilding entire communities. It is not only about rebuilding communities that have lost their churches, but about rebuilding a much larger community where people of different races and religions can live together in peace.

This chapter is largely based on *A Time to Heal: National Council of the Churches of Christ in the USA 1996–1997 Report on the Burned Churches Project.* Verification of all facts and sources of all quoted matter are on record at the National Council of Churches, Burned Churches Project, 475 Riverside Drive, New York, NY 10115.

2

"Out of Tragedy Can Come Great Joy!"
Voices from the Fire
Herb Boyd

While the African American community has experienced waves of terrorism in the past, the epidemic of burned black churches in 1996 was unprecedented. Beginning in January and during the course of the year, more than 80 African American or multiracial churches were victimized by arson attacks, and many of those fires can be directly linked to racial hatred. The images of houses of worship consumed by flames have left an indelible scar on communities from Miller, Georgia, to Portland, Oregon, and without exception the recounting of these shameful acts is never an easy one for members of the congregations or their pastors.

There is not room here to record all the gripping testimony about the fires, but three pastors who witnessed the devastation have agreed to share their plight, as well as the renewal of the hope which has emerged from the tragedies: the Rev. William Vaughan, Jr., pastor of New Shiloh and Grace United Methodist Churches in Fruitland, Tennessee, white congregations; the Rev. Terrance Mackey, pastor of Mt. Zion African Methodist Episcopal Church in Greeleyville, South Carolina; and the Rev. Robert Jeffrey, pastor of New Hope Baptist Church in Seattle, Washington.

When Mr. Jeffrey's church, New Hope Baptist, was burned in the spring of 1994, it could not have happened at a worse time. Members of the congregation, guided by Reverend Jeffrey, were active in several progressive community programs. "Ironically, the fire occurred at a time when we were involved in various social and political activities and we were trying to create a mood of tolerance in the city, especially towards our gay and lesbian community," Jeffrey recalled. "We were also working to establish a more harmonious relationship between African Americans and our Jewish sisters and brothers. To this end we had assisted in forming an African American–Jewish coalition, a coalition based on many years of cooperation and partnership.

"Of equal importance to us was economic development. We had started an African American Endowment Fund in which we asked 5,000 people in the community to put $200 into the endowment fund each year," the minister continued. "Our aim was to use the interest from the money to create business and to stimulate economic growth. The fund would provide easy access, low-interest loans to aspiring entrepreneurs who had been stifled by red-lining and unfair banking practices. Furthermore, we were involved in protests and boycotts against Safeway stores where two unarmed black men had been killed—one was shot and the other was killed in a choke hold. They were allegedly stealing from the stores. These were a few of the initiatives underway when the church was burned."

But even before the fire, there were rocks thrown through the windows of the church. "We were told that these were random acts of violence," Rev. Jeffrey said. "I have been the pastor at New Hope for eight years and we had never experienced such incidents. So, on three separate occasions the large plate glass window at the front of the church was smashed with rocks, but the police insisted they were only random acts of violence and that evidently someone in the community had something against us."

Following these incidents, Jeffrey was asked to lead a gay community march through downtown. There was at the time a growing outcry in the city from gay and lesbian persons about legislation that would abrogate their constitutional rights. "After I delivered a speech a member of the Ku Klux Klan came up to me on a bicycle to inform me that I was no longer a minister, that he had fired me," he recounted. "'I fire you,' he told me. I reported it to the police and four days later I was awakened by one of the deacons at my church who called to tell me that the alarm company had called to tell him someone was walking in the basement of the church. By the time I got there—and I only live four blocks from the church—it was completely destroyed.

Later that day we were told it was an accidental fire. To challenge that assessment was difficult since the fire chief and the investigator were African Americans, and to dispute them would be tantamount to suggesting they were incompetent or inept."

The sanctuary at New Hope was totally devastated, Jeffrey remembered. "The pews were melted to the floor," he noted. "The piano was overturned, and I spent the rest of the day in tears. Some of the neighbors described the fire to me, and one of them who lived across the street from the church said the flames shot out almost to her porch. She said she heard an explosion and was afraid her house would catch on fire. Obviously, the neighborhood was in complete shock."

But rather than pursuing the cause of the fire and risking a confrontation with the police, the fire chief—who was the first black to hold such a position in the city—and the mayor, Jeffrey decided it was best to focus his concern on his congregation. He said, "They needed me to attend to their loss and minister to their needs during this time of grief. Despite the loss of our church, the ministering had to continue and we had to keep up our campaign for economic justice. While we raised more than $40,000 for the endowment fund, we had to forgo the boycott against the Safeway stores because most of our people were involved in healing and restoration. We had to take care of the spiritual needs of our congregation before we could commit ourselves fully to the struggle over the other issues we had formerly supported.

"The spiritual reality of the church is felt in how it treats the community. One of the things that bothers me about the current position of the church is that while we witness the increased number of people returning to worship, we don't see the rise of the church's commitment to the community. For example, I frequently ask my people this question, 'If I ask you to tithe to the church, who does the church tithe to?' If members of my congregation are giving money to the church out of their secular reality then the church must give back to them. In Corinthians it talks about the relationship between the church and the minister, about members providing for his secular needs while he takes care of their spiritual needs. But it is more than taking care of the minister; it's about the role of the church and what it does to care for the community. And it is my aim to free the church from corporate dependency which makes it possible for some corporations to use the church as a tax shelter. To be involved in such ungodly things is not the spiritual mandate of the church."

Reverend Jeffrey believes these injustices and the rise of racism are connected with the abdication of responsibility to people, the responsibility that their rights be protected. "When the government and the church abdicate their responsibility," he asserted, "then a climate is created that certain people have rights and other people do not. More and more we see the denial of basic human rights in an immigration policy that treats Mexicans, for example, different from the way European immigrants were treated. This climate is conducive to the rise of skinheads, neo-Nazis and other right wing groups. One of the critical issues today is for us to purge our institutions of the need to separate, isolate, and divide people. These things must be done if we are to dissipate the climate of hatred and to achieve the beloved community that Dr. King gave his life for."

Dr. King was also recalled by Rev. William Vaughan, Jr. as he related how an aspect of his life was altered by the great "drum major" for justice. "I was preparing to go on a hunting trip when it was announced that Dr. King had been assassinated," he began. "I vowed then and there that I would never shoot a rifle again, and I have not." This pacifist tendency has formed Mr. Vaughan's political and philosophical outlook since that eventful day in 1968, and King's non-violent resolve must have been comforting that day when his church, New Shiloh, was engulfed in flames. Vaughan, who is also the pastor of Grace United Methodist Church in the same town, Humboldt, Tennessee, has been a pastor for fifty-four years.

"I received a call late one evening in 1994 that the church was on fire," said Rev. Vaughan. "By the time I got there New Shiloh was completely ablaze. There was no way to get into the church to salvage anything. People were standing around crying, and saying, 'What are we going to do?' I consoled them and told them that the church would be rebuilt. Of course, I had no idea how that would be done."

Later, Rev. Vaughan received a call from the bishop of his church who wanted to know if a merger of the two congregations, New Shiloh and Grace, could now be considered. "When I approached the congregation with the options of merging, rebuilding, or dissolving the church, thereby allowing members to join new churches, the answer was unanimous—they wanted to rebuild New Shiloh. I thought this was the right decision because I had witnessed very few effective mergers," he said. "Even so, there remained the daunting task of how to rebuild the church. All the more tragic, we had earlier on the day of the fire made the final payment on the mortgage to the 60-year-old church."

In the succeeding weeks, with reports of more houses of worship being burned, William Vaughan wondered what was going on, whether it was just a bunch of wild persons out there who had by setting the fire lost all rationality and decency. "Then I began to wonder about a conspiracy," he mused. "Let me say that I am still mystified by all the burnings. I can't comprehend what would possess someone to burn down a church. I do believe that it may have something to do with racism.

"At first I was convinced that our church was burned because someone thought it was a black church because of its proximity to Salem Baptist which is a black church. A year later Salem, too, went up in flames. But unlike our fire which was deemed accidental, the one at Salem was considered the work of an arsonist, and from that point on the federal authorities and the fire marshals began investigating the fires thoroughly."

For this and other reasons, members of Salem Baptist and New Shiloh United Methodist have developed a close relationship. In fact, the first donation New Shiloh received for the rebuilding of its church came from Salem. "And, of course, we did the same when their church was burned," the Rev. Vaughan remarked. "This mutual tragedy only deepened our ties, and when it was announced that President Clinton and Vice President Gore and their families would be coming to Humboldt to help in the rebuilding effort, the two churches pooled their resources to coordinate the event. Since then we have prayed together and shared interracial and interdenominational meetings. The pastor of Salem, Daniel Donaldson, and I are good friends and we traveled together to Washington, D.C., last June to meet with Attorney General Reno, Secretary of the Treasury Rubin, and other government officials.

"I have always believed that out of the worst tragedy something good can emerge," Rev. Vaughan continued. "We have established new friends and relationships that we might not ever have had, and practically doubled our attendance at church, so all of this is sure to help race relations in our community."

As for the rebuilding of the church, Rev. Vaughan said, "the only thing we could do at first was to start raising money, and this would have to come initially from a congregation composed of ordinary kinds of people. We have only a couple of members who might be viewed as wealthy. Things were kicked off with a benefit concert and a fish fry, and gradually the money began flowing in from various church groups." Presbyterians, Catholics, and folks from just about every denomination sent money to rebuild the church. "This was followed by teams of volunteers who came to donate their time and effort in the rebuilding process. One of our community leaders donated the land we needed to extend the church and add parking," Vaughan concluded.

"Then, like a bolt from the blue, I got a call from a reporter who wanted me to tell him about the $30,000 we had been awarded by the National Council of Churches," said Rev. Vaughan. "I told him I didn't know anything about such an award. He insisted that the church had been granted $30,000. I kept telling him that I couldn't believe it. So I got on the phone and called the NCCC's Burned Churches Project and, lo and behold, it was true. There is no way we could have completed the rebuilding of the church, which took two years, without the help of the National Council of Churches.

"As I reflect back on the church fires and their impact on me, I feel I am no less liberal politically and theologically than I was before. What they have done, though, is to convince me more than ever that we have to solve the problem of racism or we are not going to get anywhere in the church or in society. I am happy to report that some solid steps have been taken to improve race relations and toward healing our communities. I think the burning of the churches and the subsequent national attention have done a lot to focus on some of the problems tearing us apart. It is time we all faced the reality that racism is a demon, and we must find a way to remove it from our society."

This sentiment was echoed fervently by the Rev. Terrance Mackey of Mt. Zion AME Church in Greeleyville, South Carolina. Many pastors have concluded that their churches were burned because of racial hatred, and the arrest and prosecution of two young Ku Klux Klan members from Greeleyville and the complicity of two others proves that such speculation is by no means farfetched. "I was sitting in the federal courtroom listening to Arthur Haley testify about his involvement in the burning of our church," Rev. Mackey recalled. "He made it unequivocally clear that he was burning the churches as part of his plan to start a race war in America by the year 2000. During his statement he said that he would even burn down white churches if that would further the possibility of a race war."

When Haley was arrested he possessed an arsenal of weapons, including a collection of assault rifles and more than 900 rounds of ammunition. Apparently Haley and another older man had influenced two younger Klan converts to burn the churches. All were convicted of the burning of Mackey's church and also of the Macedonia Baptist Church in nearby Bloomville. "One of the young men received nineteen-and-a-half years and the other was sentenced to eighteen years," Mackey said. "So it is easy to see why so many church burnings can be attributed to racial hatred. And to fight this growing menace we can no longer apply a Band-aid like we did in the sixties. It calls for total action and that means from leaders in higher government as well as everyday kind of people that live in our community."

Many of these common folks have already put their shoulders to the wheel in the rebuilding of the Rev. Mackey's church, which was destroyed by fire in June 1995. "We rebuilt our church in exactly 360 days," Mackey said, noting the full-circle of the event. "The total cost of the rebuilding was $310,000 and the National Council of Churches Burned Churches Fund gave us $72,000." The rest of the money came via donations, insurance, and a sizable loan the congregation was able to secure.

"This community will never ever be the same," Rev. Mackey lamented. "This is a very small community [about 500 people: 300 blacks, 200 whites] and it will not be the same as it was before. I believe the fire transformed the community, and we were definitely changed after President Clinton came and recognized our tragedy. When he came, I rode with him in a car with the mayor, and we shared some things with the President—just the three of us. It was an opportunity to get on with the mayor with whom I've had differences and we bridged some gaps. I think it's a positive step in the right direction for our community."

After the fire, Mackey said he lost members of his congregation but that has been offset by the arrival of a host of new members. "Our church members were devastated following the fire," Mackey said, "and there was an offer made to merge our church with another congregation. But after the matter was discussed thoroughly, it was decided that we would stay the course and rebuild our own church."

Similar to the relationship that was formed between Pastors Vaughan and Donaldson in Tennessee, Rev. Mackey has forged strong ties with the pastor and members of Macedonia Baptist Church. "I have taken on the task of advising others about church burnings," said Mackey, who had a leadership role in a successful march against racism in Columbia, South Carolina. "Since I've been through the fire, literally and figuratively, I'm in a position to tell people about this experience, although there are some churches not interested in hearing what I have to say. Why? Because they are fearful that by having me at their church it might invite racists and others to burn their churches."

Undaunted by such refusals, Rev. Mackey has found a number of ways to help in the fight against racism and to restore communities fragmented by intolerance. "I was just at a State Senate hearing the other day," he said, "to have a law amended that would make the burning of churches a first degree crime, rather than a third degree one. I spoke to the committee and they voted the motion into law before I left the Senate."

Now Rev. Mackey has become determined to work for the removal of the Confederate battle flag from atop the State Capitol in Columbia. "It is time to bring it down and put it in the dustbin of history where it belongs," Mackey concluded.

All the key issues expressed by these three pastors were reiterated during a June 1997 convocation held in Washington, D.C., by the NCCC's Burned Churches Project. At that event these three clergy joined a number of other ministers at a roundtable discussion with Vice President Al Gore, Attorney General Janet Reno, Treasury Secretary Robert Rubin, and Housing and Urban Development Secretary Andrew Cuomo. Vice President Gore was particularly pleased to see Rev. Vaughan and Rev. Daniel Donaldson among the contingent of pastors since they are from his home state of Tennessee. He told the story of how their churches have formed a productive fellowship, worshiping and praying together whenever possible. "The fires have brought these two churches together and there's much more good that has come from this tragedy," the vice president said. "A lit match has brought us closer together."

Robert Jeffrey and William Vaughan made poignant remarks. Rev. Jeffrey, as he had done earlier during the convocation in reaction to the National Church Task Force Report, focused his statement on the continuing plague of racism. "Racism is a subtle issue," he told the pastors and government officials gathered at the Justice Department. "It's all about fear and intimidation, but we've got to move beyond these obstacles, and challenge the intolerance that attempts to nullify our unity."

Rev. Mackey confined his statement to the status of children who lost their churches through arson. "We have to do something about the younger people of these congregations whose churches have been destroyed by fire," he began. "This is often a traumatic experience and many of them need counseling."

He was also quite outspoken about restoring communities where houses of worship have been desecrated. "Sure, we can build big, beautiful new churches," he declared, "but sometimes they exist right in the middle of communities that are falling apart, crumbling down. Our communities have to be knitted back together, along with the rebuilding of new churches."

This chapter is based on taped interviews with its subjects. Original tapes or verbatim texts are on record at the National Council of Churches, Burned Churches Project.

3

Burning Churches
An Ecumenical Response
McKinley Young

In report after report, we encounter sad tales of sorrow, anguish and frustration as members of congregations which felt the heat of their beloved churches aflame, report the effect that such an action has had on church and community. "This church was over 100 years old, and we loved it so much. How could someone do this? This is an outrage that someone should so desecrate a house of God." The Reverend D. Donaldson of Fruitland, Tennessee, remarked after his church had been burned that a hurt feeling came over him which reached down in his soul. He remarked that this crisis is not new for African Americans, but there remained the hope that such an action would not happen.[1] In most cases where pastors or members of burned churches were interviewed, one could sense the anger and frustration of such actions. Not only was property destroyed, but communities were once again fragmented over issues of race and racism. Once again the ugly face of racism had raised its head and created an environment of fear, suspicion, and distrust. Why were black churches being targeted for such a holocaust? And what was going to be the recourse of these whose churches had been so ignobly razed? The questions were serious, and by the middle of 1995, a national cry could be heard to address these acts of hatred and violence in a palpable manner.

Religious affiliation throughout the country began to speak out against the hatred and racism evidenced in the church burnings. With this outrage went calls for concise and swift action by the United States government. And with over 124 churches burned by the end of 1996,[2] the problem had reached an epidemic level. Something had to be done. In response to outrage, the National Council of the Churches of Christ in the USA (NCCC) reacted by addressing the problem on two levels: "(1) to stand with the victimized congregations with pastoral care providing material support toward the goal of restoring each congregation to appropriate and needed ministries and rebuilding each destroyed building as an effective base for such service to go forward; (2) to expose and challenge the causes of those unwarranted, hate-filled and destructive acts, often giving expression to a virulent racism which continues to live as a destructive illness in our common life.[3] The Reverend Dr. Joan Brown Campbell recognized that "racism is a spiritual issue—an evil sin, acted out against God and neighbor." She noted that "we have to ask the question, 'who struck the match, and why.'" This question "why" leads to the deeper questions of why the culture of America has not seriously or adequately addressed the deeper issues of racism and prejudice in this country in an authentic and sincere manner. For well over a century, and even before, we have been tripping over this "color line."

At the turn of the century, W. E. B. DuBois made the prophetic and historically accurate statement that "the problem of the twentieth century is the problem of the color line." He understood at that time the systemic maladies that mitigate the full acceptance of African Americans into the American mainstream. Throughout this century, there have been repeated attempts by African Americans to gain full partnership in these United States. At nearly every turn, this thrust has been thwarted and the problem of the color line once again surfaces. The problems of race and racism arise and the proverbial question returns in one form or another: What shall be done with African Americans?[4] It is a hurtful question, one felt when one is tolerated, but not accepted.

From the backlash of *Plessy vs. Ferguson* which gave impetus to more legalized discrimination against African Americans, to its more virulent cousin, Jim Crow, African Americans have suffered the ravages of racism. People of African descent in America have been persecuted, harassed, lynched, and had their property vandalized or completely destroyed because an individual or organized groups felt that these blacks need to be taught to stay in their "place." And when a "place" was forged out by African Americans, there was still the sense that African Americans could not measure up and could never be fully enfranchised into the fabric of American society. The events in 1923 in the town of Rosewood demonstrate this fact. Here a town, inhabited predominately by African Americans flourishes a bit, even advances. At the pinnacle of its success, however, the city is destroyed and lives are lost when racism finds a way to raise its head and stir up the emotion of hatred and fear. In the predominately white neighboring town of Sumner, the under-currents of racism bubble until the opportune moment. In the subsequent eruption, African American property is burned, lives are lost and residents are relocated. Still, the question emerges: What shall be done with the Negroes? The answer: Kill them and burn their city down. DuBois comments: "Three centuries' through has been the raising and unveiling of that bowed human heart, and now behold a century new for the duty and the deed. The problem of the Twentieth Century is the problem of the color line."[5] It appears he was right.

This color line has traumatized the black community. Every time African Americans think that they can freely participate in the freedom of this country, something reminds them that they are black and that any achievements made or any advances experienced are suspect. The event of the church burnings is just another opportunity to challenge the problem of being black and American. It seems the moment that trust seems possible among the races, and glimmers of hope loom from sea to shining sea, an event happens such as the church burnings which leaves the black community in America understanding that the more things change, the more they stay the same. Again, DuBois captured the essence of what it has felt like and still feels like to be black and American. He states that African Americans suffer from a double-consciousness: "It is a peculiar sensation, this double-consciousness, this sense of always looking at one's self through the eyes of others, of measuring one's soul by the tape of a world that looks on in amused contempt and pity. One ever feels his 'twoness,'—an American, a Negro; two souls, two thoughts, two unreconciled strivings; two warring ideals in one dark body. . . ."[6]

The question still remains what type of climate exists which fosters an undercurrent of prejudice and hatred to the extent that these heinous acts of violence are perpetrated against members of the religious community. What seeds of unrest and hatred have germinated into acts which burn down churches whose only offense is that the congregation is predominately African American or somehow identified with similar causes?[7] Referring again to literature, I can only think that one of the reasons that these churches are such easy targets is that the attitude of the dominant culture still attributes little significance to the anguish and cry of African Americans. It is as if African Americans are invisible. If one recalls Ralph Ellison's novel *Invisible Man*, one gets a better sense of what this idea means. The main protagonist states that he is an invisible man. It was not that he was a ghost or a creature from some horror movie. "I am a man of substance, of flesh and bone, fiber and liquids— and I might even be said to possess a mind. I am invisible, understand, simply because people refuse to see me . . . . When they approach me they see only my surroundings, themselves, or figments of their imagination—indeed—everything and anything except me."[8]

Indeed, this description points to the stark reality of the way African Americans feel in America. Why would someone burn a place in the community which symbolizes hope and community? Why would hatred burn so deeply within the perpetrators of these crimes to the extent that so many churches have been burned? One answer to these questions is housed in the idea of invisibility. From a psychological point of view, it does not matter what one does to an entity that does not exist. That is how many African Americans feel about their position in this society. They are invisible. And so the dominant culture does not have to deal with overt acts of hatred toward African Americans because it does not really see a whole human being or a whole group of people who long for inclusion, for enfranchisement.

The historical record supports the fact of this notion of invisibility. At least during slavery, there was question over whether blacks were three-fourths of a human being. In the current struggle the recognition of worth diminishes to invisibility. So, if members of the dominant culture can walk by and not acknowledge the personhood of another because of that person's skin color or socio-economic level, there is fear, suspicion, and rage engendered in generations of African Americans who consequently in their own ways have gone underground in order to find some sense of self. This climate of distrust creates people who find it difficult to trust the intentions of the dominant culture toward them. Thus nothing happens in the society to ameliorate a situation which fuels hatred and distrust. In fact, what results is a climate in which, given the strained economic and racial biases, terrible acts of violence can occur. The burning of the black churches somehow reflects an underlying sense that the dominant culture may not really care about what has historically been invisible to it, i.e., African Americans. And since there has been so little concern about what happens to African Americans in this country, it has been hard to imagine even that other Christian communions from the dominant culture would rally behind moves toward the elimination of these senseless acts of racism, violence, and treachery.

What has been the response of the various church bodies regarding the church burnings? The National Council of Churches, as this book also demonstrates, has documented examples of the many contributions of its member communions. The National Council is composed of 33 church bodies who have come together to address the matter of the burned churches in a palpable manner. Each of the communions has joined with the National Council to express their outrage concerning the burning of these churches. Once again, in describing the ecumenical response to the acts of violence, Joan Brown Campbell, General Secretary of the NCCC, has stated that the twofold commitments of the Burned Church Project are (1) to support these victimized congregations in tangible ways, providing material support, and (2) to challenge the forces which give rise to racism and hatred of this sort.[9]

These 33 church bodies have by their declaration and deeds stood against the evil of racism, which Joan Campbell refers to as "an evil sin, acted out against God and neighbor."[10] Many from these churches came to the sites of the burned churches and contributed to the work necessary to restore the buildings. Others offered in-kind contributions for the building and equipping of the churches. All of these contributions gave tremendous help to those whose church facilities had been desecrated or destroyed. Indeed, there are stories after stories of how church folk from various religious groups throughout this country banded together to assist in rebuilding the burned churches. Individuals from these churches stood in solidarity with those whose *axis mundi* lay in ruin after a twilight conflagration. They were equally as outraged as the victims. And in that outrage they saw these burnings as acts of cowardice not just against those victims, but against all of humanity. Clearly, this issue seemed to cross racial lines. For a time, the feeling of invisibility did not apply in the African American community when the mainstream church bodies focused on the travesty of these burnings.

Of course there have been church burnings in this country since after the Civil War. In much of the time since then, there has been some uproar over the burnings of African American churches, but not much. Mainline church bodies may have commented on the events, but the burning of African American church buildings was not a priority issue in many places. In a country where acts of racial violence had become "business as usual" toward African Americans, it was no wonder churches could ignore the overt acts of aggression against these houses of worship. But there was something different in the responses of major church bodies regarding these recent incidents. The outcry against these actions has been more pronounced and proactive. There has been a sincerity which makes African Americans think that the lion and the lamb can truly lie beside each other in peace.

What is the difference? These crimes seemed so out of place in the 1990s. Everyone knows that racism exists, but in this era it has taken on a more covert form. The covert, institutional forms of racism, while very dangerous and detrimental, are more difficult to detect. Overt acts of hatred have in fact become anathema to many Americans, especially to the religious community. Recently, such episodes of racial and hate crimes have received much public disapproval. In the case of the burned churches, *A Time to Heal: National Council of Churches of Christ in the USA 1996–1997 Report on the Burned Churches Project* describes vividly the racism and its effects which the dominant culture has grown to abhor. "The burnings that took place between 1990 and 1997 were both violent and tragically destructive. . . . Those who set the fires intended the damage to be swift and complete, and their message to be loud and clear. Hate graffiti, such as 'kill the niggers,' 'white is right,' and the drawing of a noose around the word 'nigger' were found on smoky walls still standing among the rubble. . . . The number of fires rose dramatically in early 1995."[11] As a result of these burnings which escalated in 1995, the NCCC insisted that there be action. And from this cry for action, the Burned Churches Project was born. This project brought national attention to the church burnings. In cases where churches had been burned and little had been done to investigate the matter, the push by the Burned Churches Project spoke with a united voice against racist acts of aggression and hatred while offering needed support to those struggling small congregations that had been burned out. The voice of this large body, the NCCC, and its constituent church bodies finally got the attention of the public. The outpouring of support against these burnings has been tremendous.

Outpourings of support have come from non-Christian groups. The Burned Churches Project note contributions from "ecumenical and other Christian Community contributors which include the National Conference of Catholic Bishops, Catholic dioceses and parishes, Catholic religious communities and organizations, state and local councils of churches, World Vision, First Church of Christ Scientist, Lutheran Church Missouri Synod and Independent congregations and other Christian organizations. Interfaith partner contributors include the American Jewish Committee, Religious Action Center of Reform Judaism–Union of American Hebrew Congregations, Unitarian Universalist Associations, Islamic Circle of North America and interfaith community groups."[12]

These groups represent much of the religious community in this country. For once the African American church stands in solidarity with other church bodies to confront the ugly face of racism. For once a large number of churches from different communions recognize an affront against humanity and as a result stand up and speak out against these actions. And in this ecumenical response there are tangible contributions toward the rebuilding of these burned churches. Clearly, these actions make the "beloved community" a real possibility. Deep within the hearts of African American churches there is the hope that this ecumenical stance against these heinous acts can somehow continue in other areas of American culture.

These church burnings have given rise to some important, albeit surprising, collaborations. In June, 1996, Ralph Reed, executive director of the Christian Coalition, the conservative Christian group, indicated that he would join with African American Christians "to stem the wave of suspicious fires sweeping black churches . . . and to help affected congregations raise money to rebuild." Reed indicated that this was an attempt "toward a long-term working relationship with black churches," which he acknowledged have previously enjoyed little support from the mostly white congregations that make up the Christian Coalition. At that June meeting, Reed stated, "we come today bearing the burden of that history with broken hearts, a repentant spirit and ready hands to fight this senseless violence."[13] Here, then, is another example of a body moved to action by these church burnings. And while many disagree concerning the motives of the Christian Coalition's involvement in this issue, their participation in the outcry against the burnings cannot be denied.

African American churches have appreciated the outpouring of support which has been shown during this crisis of church burnings. The manner in which church bodies have rallied has been affirming and redeeming. There must be a God somewhere if churches that have traditionally been at odds with the causes of the African American community, and to a lesser extent with African American church communions, have taken a stand against racial violence and have contributed to the rebuilding of the burned churches. There has been evidence that culturally diverse communities have joined forces to make a positive difference in these crisis situations. Yet all of these acts, while greeted with gratitude, carry with them a wariness born out of years of disappointment and betrayal.

African American church communions wonder if the immediate actions of the dominant culture will translate into a long-term commitment of church bodies to be concerned about racial justice and reconciliation as a way of life. In the case of the contributions of the Christian Coalition, some find it difficult to trust the Coalition's motives leading to their stance regarding the church burnings. One case in point is how the Reverend Joseph Lowery responded to Ralph Reed's request to meet with African American Christians. The Reverend Lowery indicated that Reed's offer was a political move, an attempt to recruit more African Americans to his conservative political agenda. Indeed, he and others find it difficult to believe one who "helped fuel the climate of hate feeding the church fires."[14] This suspicion or wariness grows out of numerous examples of believing that the dominant culture had the best interest of African Americans in mind, only to find out later that such was not the case. So while each move to strengthen the entire community is embraced by most African American church bodies, there is still some skepticism regarding a long-term commitment by the dominant culture to liberty, freedom, and justice for all.

Further, at the heart of this crisis is the question of how we address those systemic conditions which support an environment of racial hatred and violence. The crisis at hand was and is immediate. People can respond quickly, and then be gone. But what will churches do to bring about conditions which will ultimately eliminate racial hatred? That is the most important albeit difficult task to accomplish. The question is: with all the press and publicity surrounding the church burnings, all the activity related to it, will these more far-reaching expectations be overlooked? A red herring is a fallacy which obscures the real issues by crowding other details into the picture which may result in the dilution of the prime issue. The prime issue is the elimination of the climate of racism in all aspects of the culture. That must be the focus of the entire religious community. The tangible evidences of support for the burned churches should continue, and the loud cry against these acts must persevere. But these acts cannot undercut the overall push that we have for a beloved community, a society open to diverse ideas and cultures, where grace, mercy and justice prevail for all its citizenry.

In our consideration of this phenomenon of the burned churches, we must conclude that this is another example of the shaking of foundations. The actions represent another example of our world breaking into pieces. If, after so many years of co-existing together, we still live in a climate of hatred and distrust, it would appear that there is little hope for the coming together of our community.

> The foundations of the earth do shake,
> Earth breaks to pieces,
> Earth is split in pieces,
> Earth shakes to pieces,
> Earth reels like a drunken man,
> Earth rocks like a hammock;
> Under the weight of its transgression earth falls down
> To rise no more.
>
> Isaiah 24:18c–20

Paul Tillich speaks of how in our complacency we forget about the tenuousness of our existence on this earth. He notes that the same science which contributed to this feeling of complacency is also the source of its distress. Tillich's metaphor of the shaking of the foundations is apropos here because the church burnings have once again shaken our society. These acts of racial hatred and violence have caused mass confusion. They have torn at the very fabric of our society, causing the foundations to shake. But there is a hope in the response to this upheaval, and the hope is seen in the many church bodies which have heeded the call of the Eternal to stand for the righteousness of God. They have believed that despite the burning of African American churches—or any church for that matter—God will be vindicated. Justice and truth will prevail, and the social climate making these racist acts of aggression possible will abate. Indeed, the church communions will take the leadership for creating a climate where the wicked will cease from troubling. Tillich noted that "in these days the foundations of the earth do shake." The terrible things we have seen do happen, but it is the task of all religious people to resist the temptation to be complacent. For in complacency, the nations furiously rage as has been the case in this country. "May we not turn our eyes away; may we not close our ears and our mouths! But may we rather see, through the crumbling of a world, the rock of eternity and the salvation which has no end."[15]

The author wishes to express his gratitude to the Rev. Dr. McClellon D. Cox, chaplain at the DeKalb Medical Center in Atlanta, Georgia, for his counsel and assistance in the preparation of this chapter.

Notes

1. From a Transcript by Elizabeth Farnsworth, *Politics of Hate: Background Report,* June 10, 1996.

2. Information from a statement by the Reverend Dr. Joan Brown Campbell, General Secretary of the National Council of Churches, made to the Committee on the Judiciary of the United States House of Representatives, "The Burned Church Project," March 19, 1997.

3. Ibid., p. 2.

4. DuBois, W.E.B., *The Souls of Black Folk,* II, The Dawn of Freedom, (1903)

5. Ibid.

6. DuBois, *The Souls of Black Folk,* I, (1903).

7. "Causes" here is meant to suggest those issues of liberty and economics as championed by African Americans: e.g., fair educational opportunity, equal employment and housing, equal access to all avenues of the dominant culture, fair exchange of ideas, etc.

8. Ellison, Ralph, *Invisible Man* (New York: Signet Books, 1952), p. 7.

9. Joan Brown Campbell, op. cit., p. 2

10. Ibid., p. 3

11. *"A Time to Heal: National Council of Churches of Christ in the USA 1996–1997 Report on the Burned Churches Project,* p. 6.

12. Ibid., p. 28.

13. "Christian Coalition Plans to Cooperate With Black Churches to Squelch Fires; Some Black Leadership Boycott Meeting," *The Washington Post,* June 19, 1996.

14. Ibid.

15. Paul Tillich, *The Shaking of the Foundations* (New York: Charles Scribner's Sons, 1948), p. 11.

4

The Cultural Conspiracy and the Black Church Fires

Jesse L. Jackson, Sr.

Whenever one mentions or uses the word conspiracy in American politics and culture, your allies run for cover, while detractors declare you paranoid—but as we all know, just because you're paranoid doesn't mean they're not out to get you.

A conspiracy is when two or more people plot in secret for the demise of someone or something. The word conspiracy has been attached to many of the conditions endured by African Americans—from disproportionate incarceration rates to unequal treatment by lenders, from the high infant mortality rate to discrimination in housing.

The fact of the matter is that the American playing field has yet to be leveled, due in large part to the lingering effects of structural and institutional racism. It is the lingering structural and institutional racism that ordinarily makes the issue of conspiracy moot. When there is all-but-total control there is little need to conspire. It is simply a matter of maintaining the status quo.

The quest for justice in America involves challenging those who would maintain a status quo with a glass ceiling above, and no floor below, for those of a particular race or sex. Needless to say, while the word conspiracy may be inappropriately used at times, it often strikes at the core of the American problem— the few unjustly benefitting at the expense of the many, while maintaining a position of entitlement and privilege by encouraging division, infighting, and animosity amongst the various groups in society. It is the age-old tactic of divide-and-conquer, which leads to scapegoating and "playing the blame game." This is what the cultural conspiracy is all about—playing the blame game.

The cultural conspiracy is the perception of a common cause for the widespread societal attacks on racial, ethnic, religious, or sexual minorities on a variety of fronts. It is often the product of respectable leaders of mainstream political and cultural institutions who offer up programs and policies doomed to failure because they fail to fully address *dispossession*. This creates intergroup resentment and blame. Those who subscribe to this implicit cultural conspiracy see what others regard as independent events as the *effects* of a common *cause*.

At night, the enemies of civil rights strike in white sheets, burning their fires. By day, they strike in black robes and blue suits, burning opportunities. The year of 1996 looked a lot more like 1896 every day. The gains of the Second Reconstruction by Dr. Martin Luther King, Jr. are being rolled back, just like Jim Crow rolled back the gains of the First Reconstruction. The Supreme Court in 1896 ruled on *Plessy vs. Ferguson,* with the idea of "separate but equal." The Supreme Court now puts out ruling after ruling under the pretense that after four centuries of slavery and government-sanctioned apartheid, with a white population which makes up 75 percent of the population, and an African American electorate which makes up only 12 percent, that everyone now operates on an equal playing field.

The notion that equal opportunity, due process, equal protection under the law, and economic justice for all come at the expense of the majority population is indeed misguided. This fatally flawed concept feeds the cultural conspiracy and fuels the anger which results in attacks against the black church.

As Justice John Paul Stevens stated, "A majority's attempt to enable the minority to participate more effectively in the process of democratic government should not be viewed with the same hostility that is appropriate for oppressive and exclusionary abuses of political power." Fair participation in governance, as well as inclusion in the economic and social structures of society, makes for a more stable society, insures our domestic tranquility, and provides for the common welfare.

However, beyond what has become a standard feature of American politics—playing the blame game—the crucial question is whether there was or remains an organized conspiracy to create terror in the African American community. And, if so, by whom and why?

Surely, the revelations of conspiracy around the Tuskegee syphilis experiment and the allegations of conspiracy made in the *San Jose Mercury News* stories about Central Intelligence Agency (CIA) and Drug Enforcement Agency (DEA) involvement in the crack epidemic in the black community warrant concern about evil plotters. In both examples, the concern is for plotters using a cover of government authority and legitimacy.

In addition, millions of Americans continue to find it difficult to believe that the assassination of Dr. King was the act of a lone hater, especially with the hate that FBI Director J. Edgar Hoover held toward Dr. King. Millions will never believe that James Earl Ray had the motive, the money, or the method to carry out Dr. King's assassination by himself.

The sense of an organized conspiracy around the church fires is intuitive. Those who attempted to address the conspiracy question generally fell into three categories. First, there were those who immediately dismissed any racial motivation behind the arsons. This group, filled with false pride in their artificial color blindness, considered the fires as unrelated acts of vandalism with little or no political or racial significance.

After a night in Louisiana in which four black churches were burned to the ground, one Bureau of Alcohol, Tobacco, and Firearms (BATF) agent reportedly added insult to injury by telling the victims that "race was not a factor," and that the only link between the Louisiana fires and fires in other states was "they were churches and they had a fire."

These kinds of statements fed those who charge conspiracy in the textbook sense of the word, who saw an organized plot—the second group. They view the acts of terrorism, violence, and intimidation against the black church—the symbolic center of African American culture—as representing an organized plot, a campaign of political and social destabilization.

This group had more than ample reason to be overcome by conspiratorial inclinations. When a pattern emerged around the burning of black churches, the cry of conspiracy was summarily dismissed or ignored by many in law enforcement. If a conspiracy existed, law enforcement officials, such as those at the BATF, initially aimed, as chapters one and two in this book point out, their suspicions at those victimized by the destruction of their own houses of worship.

In certain criminal investigations, especially arson, it is common for law enforcement officials to question the alleged victims as well as the suspects. The Susan Smith murder case is an example as to why this is important—sometimes, things are not as they seem. The omnipresence of the cultural conspiracy allowed a sick mother to initially claim that a black man had abducted her two children. Still, after the facts are gathered, law enforcement officials should use common sense in the search for truth. This did not seem to be the case when investigating the black church fires. Stereotyping and insensitivity replaced common sense. It has been widely reported that church members and pastors were given on occasion repeated lie detector tests, implying that they were engaged in a criminal plot to burn their own churches down to collect insurance money. Because of the ongoing cultural conspiracy with its stereotyping and scapegoating, blacks were the first suspects regardless of the fact that, as the NCCC Burned Churches Project Report indicates, many of the churches torched were either underinsured or uninsured.

Suspicion of the BATF also arose from the crisis. News organizations revealed that several BATF and FBI agents had participated in the racist "Good Ole' Boy Roundup." Many of the agents attending this "whites only" event were also in charge of several of the bombing investigations. There was a cycle of mistrust. Sympathetic media coverage and political pressure forced investigative agencies to change their approach in dealing with the victims.

However, civil rights leaders, ministers, and church members reflected back to the 1960s, when Federal agencies often infiltrated hate groups to gather information. Many could conceive that the reverse had happened in the 1990s, that "the fox was guarding the hen house." For the most part, the "non-racial" assumptions of the BATF were dismissed by most African Americans.

Those worried about an organized plot offered up the fact that in the earlier investigations, most of those arrested for the arsons were white males whose ages ranged from the teens to the mid-forties. Furthermore, many of those charged are generally alleged to have been members of the various state "Realms" within the Invisible Empire of the Ku Klux Klan, the Aryan Faction, and the Skinheads for White Justice. African American leadership's concern grew from an environment so poisonous that, in Tennessee, a lodge was firebombed and a black furniture store manager was killed when his car was bombed after he was alleged to have been dating white women. In an environment where ministers were receiving death threats, and the perpetrators were scrawling racist graffiti, such as "kill all niggers" on the walls of churches, the fear of an organized plot was validated for many.

Additionally, it is an acknowledged fact that most of the churches attacked were isolated, rural settings with high concentrations of poor and working class blacks. In the past, this was a common Klan trait. But rural, southern African Americans were not the only victims. As is often the case, blacks were simply the weathervane signaling what was just ahead for the rest of society. We are the first to get wind of what is going on in the society as a whole; and if poisonous cultural gases are in the air, we are the first to breathe them.

In this case, those who traditionally seek common ground with African Americans were also attacked by racists. To fail to recognize their pain is to fall victim to the divide-and-conquer tactic. It is known that: a white church in Georgia was bombed after its pastor spoke out against cross burnings. Jewish synagogues in the North and Midwest were attacked as were several interracial congregations in the West and Northwest; in the Massachusetts synagogue fires, four Skinheads were convicted.

The churches in the Northwest which were burned advocate interracialism and gay rights in the region designated by The Order, a splinter group of the Aryan Nations, as "the last bastion of white predominance." The Order of the Aryan Nations has adopted *The Turner Diaries,* by William Pierce, as its manifesto of the "coming race war." *The Turner Diaries,* which became infamous during Timothy McVeigh's trial in Oklahoma City, is the story of a "right-wing" white revolution, and of an underground group called The Order, which spearheads the rebellion against blacks, Jews, interracial couples, and the government which "protects" them. In this book, the racists are the "good guys."

Perhaps coincidentally, those claiming responsibility for the Atlanta clinic and gay night club bombings have been reported by the press to refer to themselves as the "Army of God" and to express their resentment against the "New World Order." (Ironically, the phrase "New World Order" gained popular notoriety after then-President George Bush used it following the Persian Gulf War.)

So, the feeling of an organized plot emerging from the church-burning crisis comes as no surprise. We would be naive, as well as unprepared, if we did not at least recognize that these organizations exist, that they stockpile weapons and explosives, and that they have an immoral mission aimed at our destruction. These people simply do not want blacks (as well as other "locked-out" Americans) around them. These are the haters, and what they feel goes well beyond the blame game. Consequently, we would be unwise not to form and maintain coalitions with those others who are the designated targets of these haters, as well as those victimized by contemporary scapegoat politics.

In any case, there is little documented (or shared) evidence that would indicate a communication or planning network amongst the various parties arrested, charged, and convicted around the country for the church fires. Conspiracies do take place, but usually, as was the case with the Texaco executive whose racist ramblings were taped, one has to be lucky to uncover such plots, or someone has to confess.

The common chord of the church-burning fires is the demagogic poison that fills the air. It is an air of perceived *winners* and *losers*. It is an air of scapegoating and stereotyping. It is the blame game. The burning of churches, the defacing of synagogues and mosques is the last stage of cultural terrorism. The black church fires prove that this is a time to fight back, not surrender.

Those in the third group, trying to address why this poisonous air exists, offer the theory of the "cultural conspiracy." The new millennium offers African American leadership the opportunity to redefine mission and focus. It is also time to demand a public policy and a public environment that does not lead to an anti-black, fascist mania. With this rededication and refocus, the church remains the symbolic center of the African American community.

To us, the fires represented a growing war to counter our efforts to end the blame game. The fires and the attacks represent a negative response to our demand for equity and parity. Racism, race politics, scapegoating, pandering, posturing, partisanship, the performance of Federal and state law enforcement agencies (and the behavior of individual agents), and allegations of conspiracy, were all interactive variables in what former U.S. Assistant Attorney General for Civil Rights Deval Patrick labeled an "epidemic of terror." Nonetheless, just as the 1963 bombing of the 16th Street Baptist Church in Birmingham, Alabama, in which four young black girls were murdered, focused national attention on a systemic campaign waged by the Ku Klux Klan, we must now turn pain into action. Working with our allies—such as the NCCC—the Rainbow/PUSH Coalition must turn pain into power.

In a real sense, the fires represent random but widespread expressions of deeply rooted racial hatred which have bubbled to the top in a cauldron of social unrest scorched by the flames of social policies which target political and economic *effects* on African Americans rather than the root *cause* of those effects.

The situation is far more serious than the activity of any organized hate group. We are not only dealing with the forces that wear white sheets, but those in black robes and blue suits who are rolling back the public policy gains of the civil rights movement. Their efforts made 1996 look like 1896—the end of the Second Reconstruction.

While the California initiatives undermining affirmative action for women and minorities, and attacking Hispanic immigrants—Propositions 209 and 187—have captured the national spotlight, these types of rollbacks are happening all across the country, and the effects have been immediate and devastating. As just one example, at the University of California School of Law at Berkeley, one of the nation's premier law schools, only one African American will be part of the law school's 272-member class in the fall of 1997. This is the direct effect of Proposition 209. The University of Texas anticipates similar results, due to the Hopwood case.

There may not be a conscious conspiracy but the fires were causally connected by the politics and policies that help perpetuate racial fear and prejudice in the minds of whites.

Evidence of the cultural conspiracy is easy to detect and identify. Those of us alarmed by attacks on holy ground hold the view that similar incidents have a causal connection—be it the actions of the courts, demagogic utterances from politicians, or the hate-filled rantings of radio talk show hosts. The cultural conspiracy is the interweaving of issues that create a blanket of hate and hostility. It is embodied in a panoply of issues from educational tracking and the debate around affirmative action and welfare, to so-called "tough on crime" legislation and California's anti-immigrant Proposition 187.

The common denominator in the blame game is the misguided and untrue notion of black *winners* and white *losers*. For persons seeking to have their racist attitudes validated in some way, mere political debate on such issues is seen as a signal okaying acts of violence. For racists, acts of physical violence and intimidation are validated by the perception of state and institutional suppression of a particular group. Stereotyping and scapegoating are key ingredients in a recipe for hostility. A member of one hate group in the South when asked why his group might support the burning of a black church was reported by the press to have replied, "That is where they learn to get on welfare. Have you ever noticed that when there is free cheese or milk and stuff, we don't know anything about it but they are the first in line?"

The reality is that most poor people are not on welfare; most poor people work every day. And most people on welfare are not black or brown—they are white, female, and two-thirds of them are children.

Since the Reagan presidency a black mask has covered the white face of poverty, and the myth that has endured is that of the black "welfare queen." Many believe that the welfare ranks are swollen with lazy black women who refuse to work in order to have babies so that they can collect money from hard-working whites. As I have pointed out many times, blacks make up less than one-third of the welfare rolls, but are highlighted in perhaps two-thirds of the media coverage on the issue. In a public atmosphere where New York radio announcer Bob Grant can call welfare mothers "maggots" and get away with it, it is no great leap for many blacks to believe that some Klan member in South Carolina, Georgia, Tennessee, Washington state, or any other area, is going to feel that burning down a house of God is somehow a sanctioned and twistedly noble act.

Media coverage of the fires focused on black churches in the South. South Carolina was prominent because of its high number of arsons and racial incidents over the past two years. Many see a nexus between the flying of the Confederate flag, the symbol adopted by the Ku Klux Klan, on South Carolina's statehouse dome, and the spreading of violence. The flag continues to represent the state's condoning a long history of white supremacy.

Beyond the focus on the fires, there was very little concern expressed over earlier incidents that were indicative of the cultural conspiracy's trend toward violence. Several examples recently reported in the press come to mind. First also in South Carolina, was the case of a white couple charged with lynching, after attacking a nine-year-old black boy when he visited their home to play with their children. Also, during the same period a black man, driving with his spouse who happened to be white, was harassed and killed by two white men who took exception to his marital preference. This was followed by national bemusement with The Redneck Shop in Laurens, South Carolina. This racist shop, with coffins in its display window containing black mannequins with nooses around their necks, needed little interpretation.

In partisan politics, the best-known expression of the idea that blacks are getting ahead at the expense of whites is the infamous Jesse Helms' "Hands" commercial, in which a pair of white hands crumple up a job rejection letter while a disappointed voice blames affirmative action (political consultant Dick Morris, former Bill Clinton advisor, used to take credit for producing the "Hands" ad). However, white women have benefited as much, if not more, from affirmative action as blacks, and the blue collar jobs that are no longer available were taken by corporate barracudas to China and Indonesia, not by the blacks and browns that Bob Dole "saw" standing on the street corners as he drove to the Senate in his limousine through Washington, D.C.

The cultural conspiracy sends many different and seemingly contradictory messages. There is the message or illusion of a "level playing field." There is also the "Blacks are responsible for their own poverty" illusion. And, there is the illusion that African Americans and other minorities have gained unfair advantage over whites through affirmative action.

The idea of proportional representation in a democracy never enters into the debate. Under a barrage of fear-mongering and downright lies, white America is told that there are bunches of government set-aside programs filled with quotas of unqualified minorities who take jobs away from universally qualified white males.

False claims of economic parity are spouted, despite the Glass Ceiling Report and other statistics to the contrary. The truth has been obfuscated, as politicians and demagogues pander to so-called "angry white males." The cycle of victimization is then complete—white males are being promoted as society's principal victims. The clouds of this transformation were seeded with scapegoat politics. The ads, messages, and illusions serve as examples of the manipulation of racial cues which promote the notions of *black winners at the expense of white losers,* and *white victims at the hands of black criminals*—despite all facts to the contrary.

Many politicians, Democrat and Republican, liberal and conservative, exploit the cultural conspiracy. Politicians often benefit from a culture of division and fear because it allows them to choose a constituency and play to press their hot buttons. Group and individual voting traits are used to carve out power niches. It is called "us against them."

In today's political culture, instead of leading, politicians take polls to see what buttons to press. The mainstream press validated and trumpeted the 1994 mid-term election as a "victory" for "angry white males." The characterization "angry white males" maintained its saliency until the Oklahoma bombing tragedy.

But what do white males really have to be angry about? According to the U.S. Census Bureau (1990):

- A black male with 4 or more years of college makes an average of $32,145 per year. A white male with the same college credentials makes an average of $41,661 (a gap of $9,500!). Are white males mad about that?
- White males make up only ⅖ of the workforce. Yet they hold 95% of the senior management positions in corporations, 80% of the U.S. House of Representatives, 90% of the U.S. Senate, 92% of the Forbes 500 list, 92% of school superintendents, 80% of tenured professors, 99.9% of professional athletic team owners, and 100% of U.S. Presidents. Are they mad about that?
- Women still make only 72% as much as men. The average income of a Hispanic woman with a college degree is less than that of a white male with a high school diploma. Hispanic men earn only 64% of white men's income. Blacks and browns are three times as likely to be poor as whites. Are white males angry about that?

We understand the pain of losing your job to corporate downsizing and outsourcing, and the anger that results. But these jobs are not being lost to affirmative action; they're being sent overseas by corporate barracudas looking for cheaper labor markets.

However, despite the fact of unfair power and wealth distribution, and corporate downsizing, the perception of black winners and white losers continues to be spread throughout American society, often by politicians looking for electoral advantage. The politics of using fear and division did not start with Strom Thurmond or Jesse Helms. The politics of fear and division, which includes race politics, has been part of American politics since the time when enslaved Africans were declared three-fifths human for census purposes.

Ronald Reagan announcing his candidacy in Philadelphia, Mississippi (at the suggestion of then-Congressman Trent Lott), the same town where civil-rights workers Schwerner, Goodman, and Chaney were murdered, was race-fear politics. Richard Nixon's "law and order" slogans, and his use of the crime issue against blacks, was also race-fear politics. George Bush's use of the "Willie Horton ad" was race-fear politics. In the 1992 election, candidate Bill Clinton outflanked the Republicans in the race-crime-fear game. He executed Ricky Ray Rector, despite his brain damage, and condemned rapper Sister Souljah in a sophisticated Democratic Leadership Conference (DLC) version of the "Willie" Horton ploy. Moreover, many remember Clinton's sojourn to Stone Mountain, Georgia, the second home of the Ku Klux Klan, to take a picture with Sam Nunn in front of a phalanx of black prison inmates. It is all part of the fear, "us against them" blame game that feeds the anti-black mania.

Step one in the fear game is easy—attack anything different, especially any group with a limited ability to fight back. Conflict is then inherent because this country, this nation of immigrants and slaves and Native Americans and Latino/Hispanics, is built on difference. America is not a melting pot, but a quilt of many colors. Yet many of these attacks come under the guise of "democracy," or what Lani Guinier calls "the tyranny of the majority."

Call it multiculturalism, diversity, the mosaic or the quilt, the differences make America unique. Yet in the current fearmania, differences are exploited through the use of a mass illusion such as the "mantra of family values." Under this illusion, everyone who does not have a family that looks, acts, and lives "thus so" is ostracized and vilified. This is one of the ways the country was induced to accept the scapegoating of blacks, Latinos, Arabs, welfare mothers, single parents, immigrants, prison inmates, and anybody that seems to differ from Rush Limbaugh's famous "ditto-heads."

Perennial presidential candidate and television personality Pat Buchanan has claimed "cultural dilution," an updated argument descended from the old fears of miscegenation or race-mixing. Historically, miscegenation in society brought protest from members of supremacy groups such as the Ku Klux Klan. Now we have more "respectable" leaders calling for racial and ethnic cleansing, with the idea seriously considered.

Plenty of organizations have documented the resurgence of hate crimes, and the Oklahoma City tragedy makes the increase in terrorist activities of racist groups obvious. Episodes of violence by those who view themselves as losing out to African Americans, or some other group, are predictable outgrowths of the blame game and fear politics. Consequently, the murder of a black couple in Fayetteville, North Carolina, by three members of the 82nd Airborne Division stationed at Fort Bragg is viewed as evolving from the cultural conspiracy. In addition, the discovery that the three convicted murderers were also members of a neo-Nazi organization, and the resulting federal inquiry into hate-group infiltration of the military, reinforced the belief, by some, of an organized conspiracy against African Americans.

The anti-black mania has been building for a long time. On a pseudo-intellectual front, the cultural conspiracy is exemplified by books such as *The Bell Curve* and proposals for racial genetic testing to determine predisposition to criminal behavior or other innate inferiority. Such voodoo science is meant to imply that black virtue and success are abnormal and that blacks must be controlled and subsidized at the expense of whites.

On the legal front, the cultural conspiracy sanctions racially disparate drug sentencing, which bloats the black prison population. In this conspiracy, black drug users are frequently given harsher sentences for crack cocaine than whites using much more powdered cocaine. The results are both predictable and sinister: prisons have become the #1 growth industry in urban America, and I have declared it a "state of emergency" that "one-third of young African Americans are caught up in the criminal justice system—either in jail, on parole, or on probation, with the consequence that one-seventh of this nation's African American males are ineligible to vote."

To many, these affronts constitute a conspiracy to incarcerate blacks to "prevent" violence. This permits police departments to "profile" and stop black drivers of expensive cars and treat them as criminal suspects. As African Americans witnessed the recent on-camera assault of a black female motorist by a South Carolina highway patrolman, many wondered when would it be their turn? The assumption by most blacks is that there are plenty of racist police for whom "driving while black" or "DWB" affords reasonable enough suspicion to turn a routine traffic stop into a life-or-death situation. The stereotype is that an African American woman driving alone on I-95 who will not stop for police is a drug courier, rather than a woman traveling alone who is afraid to stop in an isolated place.

The haunting question remains as to whether race-hatred symbolism was directly connected to the church bombings and racial attacks. Possibly, though no conscious conspiracy or network of well-organized plotters has been uncovered. However, the persistence of widespread racial hatred and fear, in the minds of many whites who are scapegoating their own exclusion from the new global economy, is all that is necessary to create the illusion of a conscious conspiracy.

Widespread racial fear of blacks is perpetuated by policies which criminalize the sort of activity (traffic in illegal substances) that naturally abounds in an economically suppressed subculture, and which escalates the level of violence normally associated with such activity. Central to the "cultural conspiracy" are plantation-style welfare and affirmative action programs which are misdirected at the twin decoys of *poverty* and *disenfranchisement* rather than at the appropriate target of *dispossession.*

While there have been some past public policy successes, the human rights movement has always struggled with the handicap that American public policy and attitudes toward dealing with the widespread poverty and unfair disenfranchisement of blacks, have more often than not ignored the root of the problem, which is *dispossession.* In economic terms, poverty is defined as substandard consumption. In political terms, disenfranchisement is substandard political power. Both are due to the lingering effects of dispossession, which is substandard ownership of capital. Consequently, dispossession is the root cause of poverty and disenfranchisement.

Progressive, and for the most part liberal, support of affirmative action programs is a matter of record. American society must take positive steps—affirmative actions—so that African Americans can gain equity and parity. Nonetheless, we must be mindful that affirmative action policy is a conservative remedy which falls far short of ending dispossession, and is in many respects a "restitution-avoidance" policy.

Dr. King called for "a radical restructuring" of American society. To this point, his challenge of radical, fundamental change has yet to be realized by our nation. Dr. King's name and image are frequently uttered and coopted without the realization or practice of his theology and ideology. It is symbolism over substance.

With this in mind, restitution avoidance, with all it engenders, is far more effective than the Helms' "Hands" commercials or Bush's Willie Horton ads at fostering the notion of *black winners at the expense of white losers,* thereby perpetuating racism in our society.

For those who rank the protection of vested interest and the status quo above the realization of justice, continuing to treat the symptoms of poverty and disenfranchisement seems easier than finding a cure for the disease of dispossession. This is due to the fact that dispossession is deeply rooted in the legacy of government-sanctioned slavery, democratically-approved Jim Crow laws, and state-sponsored apartheid.

Our movement has at times been at odds about strategies for confronting dispossession. If the country was in denial about its original sin of racism, and its deep-rooted structures of discrimination, how could we make them realize that a debt was owed African Americans? Thus, a major emphasis of the civil-rights movement of the 1960s was the struggle for opportunity. The civil rights movement was dedicated to attaining equal protection, due process, equal opportunity, and economic fairness for all. However, while equal opportunity is necessary, it alone is not sufficient to establish racial justice. When the phrase "justice denied" is raised in the context of American history, it refers to those particular human rights denied on the basis of race or gender.

As America moves to the next millennium, the civil rights community must renew its commitment to protecting and advancing human rights. Our struggle is the attainment of social, economic, and political justice for all Americans—and the end of privilege for a chosen few. For African Americans, this means that we must embrace the abolitionists' goal of "forty acres and a mule"—meaning that former slaves and their heirs should be given restitution in the form of private ownership of capital and the means of production.

The problem of dispossession has not been effectively addressed by bureaucratically administered welfare or affirmative action strategies. Many young people now mistakenly believe that the goal of the civil rights movement was welfare and affirmative action, because whenever these issues arise, pictures of black people abound. Although blacks are disproportionately poor, this, more often than not, is due to dispossession.

The current system of welfare arose out of the Great Depression—Franklin Delano Roosevelt passed the New Deal to counteract white poverty. Welfare is part of the safety net of a humane society. This is not to say that welfare should replace effort; people do not want a handout, but they do need a helping hand up. Welfare was not a specific goal of the civil rights movement; we marched for jobs and justice.

We sought opportunities and fair treatment for the poor and dispossessed. In the 1960s, we believed that it was better for our society to spend tax money on priorities here at home rather than financing a jungle of death known as the Vietnam War. As for affirmative action, it was the conservative remedy meant to mollify. And now, they are attempting to reverse the little that we won. It is time for us to demand more, rather than accepting retrogression.

Three decades after the civil rights movement, 40 percent of the descendants of slaves remain dispossessed, second-class citizens in conditions of dependency, and under attack. While we advocate protection of the social safety net, this does not mean that we believe the sole solution to the problem of the 40 percent is welfare. The solution is real opportunities.

Conservative politicians offer us empty slogans like "equal opportunity" to compete in the global marketplace, without the capital, education, job training, or social support systems necessary for fair competition. Liberal politicians make false promises of "equal opportunity" in education, while not dealing with the resegregation and unfair funding of public schools; or "affordable housing," which at this point in our history seems to be contained within the jail-industrial complex; or "access" to medical care, under the domination of the medical, drug, and insurance industries, and without the means to pay for it.

Conservatives tell African Americans that their problems are of their own making or are due to genetic predisposition. They extol minorities to "pick themselves up by the bootstraps" of their non-existing boots. While conservatives—and too many liberals—vote to move government toward "privatization," to give away the broadcasting spectrum, to sell off huge tracts of profitable public land, and to bail out millionaires who lost money in the S&L scandal, they continue to renege on those in the first debtor position—the descendants of slaves.

There may not be an organized conspiracy to commit sense-less acts of racial violence against blacks and black institutions in America, but there is a highly organized conspiracy behind the persistence of racial fear and hatred that fuel those acts of violence. Liberals and conservatives, Republicans and Democrats have ignored the pain of dispossession while instituting policies which have trapped all but the most courageous, enterprising, and fortunate African Americans in conditions of dependence. Public policies have fostered the illusion that black gains come at the expense of whites, thus enabling many whites to scapegoat their own victimization by increasingly global corporate predators, thereby ensuring the persistence of a divide-and-conquer political strategy in America. Racism, with its ingrained fear and hatred, leads to the burning of churches.

America is moving toward the end of this century with the same tragic music with which *Plessy vs. Ferguson* ended the last century. Many see more trouble just around the bend. Fear and distrust in the justice system is why African Americans can easily believe that a Los Angeles police officer might plant a bloody glove. Fear inspires burning schools in Mississippi and bombing buildings in Oklahoma City. We can expect violence in a political climate where fear is exploited to pit "righteous angry victims" against one another. Honest public discourse is the only antidote to future unrest. The media and politicians at every level, from the President to the city councillor to the local school board, can help reverse the trend of fear, hatred, cynicism, and violence by decoding racist code words, and by evaluating legislation according to its disparate racial effects.

We know that welfare, urban crime, and "black" have been used as synonymous political terms. That is the basis for African Americans being made objects of vilification grossly over-represented in the jail-industrial complex. That is the basis for African Americans being seen as less intelligent, less hard-working, less universal, less patriotic, and more violent than we are.

President Clinton's "National Conversation on Race" is a welcome starting point for addressing these issues. Institutional racism, however, is more than deep-seated—it is about political power used to maintain a privileged economic position. Dealing with structural inequality, power, and privilege will require an "apology" by America, an attempt to "repair," and a real "remedy." In addition, we must define what "apology" and "repair" and "remedy" really mean to African Americans, as we enter the 21st century.

Racism is difficult to address and redress. Redress demands the pursuit of truth and an uncompromising quest for justice. It costs money, and it requires government—not just volunteer—action. Solving the problem of racism is about challenging the notion of entitlement to privilege and changing the nature of institutions which protect such privilege. Dr. King referred to it as "speaking truth to power." In the current culture, it is chic to use buzzwords that denote a certain sincerity or religiosity such as "reconciliation," "redemption" and "repentance"; but without the fourth R, "restitution," this is only empty sincerity and false religiosity.

Finally, African Americans must be clear in their desire for inclusion. Our struggle is about securing equal protection under the law, equal opportunity, due process, and economic justice for all those who have been institutionally harmed and shut out. We want to be included in a "one big tent" America. This was Dr. King's dream. And until we are truly "one nation," we must continue Dr. King's struggle.

The author is grateful to Kevin Alexander Gray for his assistance in the preparation of this chapter.

5

The Burning of Churches and the Communion of Churches

Philip Turner

I

The National Council of Churches estimates that by the end of the summer of 1996 some 90 houses of worship had been "attacked, desecrated, vandalized, and burned" as the result of "racially motivated hate."[1] By the end of that same year, the number had risen to 124. In response, the Council began the Burned Churches Project. Through its efforts and those of other non-profit and governmental organizations, some $25 million in resources came "to focus on the epidemic of church burnings."[2]

If the burning of these churches testifies to the continuing presence of hate and racism in America, the generous response that came from so many quarters testifies both to the disgust these evils evoke in the American public and to their willingness to come to the aid of the victims of racially motivated hatred. The Burned Churches Project drew forth a remarkable response. It harnessed the efforts and resources of individuals, churches and synagogues, government agencies, corporations, foundations, and non-profit organizations.

The intentions and motives of the various individuals and bodies involved in this effort no doubt vary as do their obligations. In the pages that follow no effort will be made to investigate or analyze what these motives, intentions, and obligations might be. It is enough to say that all individuals and groups involved in the effort were appalled by these acts of violence and all wanted to offer moral support and concrete help. The purpose of this essay is not to ask about what the motives, intentions, and obligations of the citizenry in general are or ought to be, but to ask, in cases like this one, how individual Christians and their churches ought to understand their own efforts to provide relief.

In search of an answer, if one is to be faithful to Christian belief and practice, it is impossible to bypass the question of what motives, intentions, and actions the *koinonia* or communion of the church might imply or mandate in circumstances like the ones surrounding the burning of these houses of worship. Reflection on the nature of the communion Christians enjoy one with another, in cases like these, leads in turn to another question—one that is both difficult and controversial. Given the nature of the *koinonia* of the church, are the intentions, motives, and actions that are appropriate for or required of Christians who find themselves in situations like these distinct in any way from those appropriate for or required of the general public? Or, to put the matter another way, are there circumstances in which Christians have particular responsibilities toward fellow believers which they might not have toward people who do not share their faith?

II

The above questions (or ones that are closely related) present themselves as much in the Middle East as they do in the Southeast of the United States. They are questions that are as alive in China as in Chattanooga. Many say that the outpouring of support for the black congregations that have been the victims of arson provides a wonderful example of the *koinonia* of the church in operation. If this is so, what does this partnership or communion imply in a normative sense about the intentions, motives, and obligations that ought at least to stand behind these expressive actions?

There are at least three narratives in the New Testament that suggest an answer; the sharing of possessions referred to in Acts (Acts 2:42–47; 4:32–37), the collection for the poor in Jerusalem mentioned in Corinthians and Romans (2 Cor. 8 and 9; Rom. 15:26–29), and the Lukan account of Peter's vision in which he is commanded to eat foods the Jews deemed unclean (Acts 10:9–33). A careful examination of these three stories will reveal a good deal both about the nature of the church's communion and the sort of motives, intentions, and obligations that constitute and support that communion.[3] They will as well provide a lens through which to discover, by analogy, how Christians ought to view their participation (or lack thereof) in the Burned Churches Project.

The classic place to begin an investigation of the *koinonia* of the church is Acts 2:42. After describing the descent of the Holy Spirit and the first apostolic preaching, Luke comments that those who responded through repentance and amendment of life, "continued in the apostles' teaching and fellowship [*koinonia*], the breaking of the bread and the prayers." He immediately follows this comment by noting that the members of this original community had all things in common (Acts 2:44). Luke goes on to make it clear that their sharing of goods was completely voluntary (Acts 4:32—5:11). Having all things in common was not a condition of membership but a freely undertaken practice expressing the fact that those who believed were of "one heart and soul." A close reading of the text will reveal that their economic arrangement was understood neither as an act of benevolence nor as an arrangement prompted by a belief that the world would soon end. Rather, it is presented as an act intended to express the inward reality that bound the community together. This inward reality was a unity of spirit born of faith in Christ which itself had been evoked by the apostolic preaching and the gift of the Holy Spirit. Indeed, this entire section of the Act of the Apostles is intended to show, among other things, that the *koinonia* of the church, in one important way, is discontinuous with all other forms of human community. Its origin is from God rather than the usual bases of human solidarity. The condition of membership is not language, race, tribe, nation, or family but a common faith in Christ that leads to repentance, newness of life, mutual love, and the exchange of goods and gifts.

This narrative suggests, therefore, that the intentionality and motivation that lie behind this original expression of *koinonia* is, in the first instance, generated by the Christian gospel itself. Though the sharing of goods was certainly intended to ensure that within the communion of the church there would be no needy person, Luke makes clear that the primary purpose of the action was to show forth in a most immediate and concrete

Flames engulf St. Paulus Lutheran Church at Eddy and Gough Streets in San Francisco early Sunday morning, Nov. 5, 1995. The fire completely gutted the church, built in 1894 and a survivor of the devastating 1906 earthquake.

(AP Photo/Antioch Ledger-Dispatch, Kendra Luck)

Burned pages of a religious book are scattered in the remains of the Rising Star Baptist Church on Tuesday, June 10, 1996 in Greensboro, Ala.

Firefighters spray water on the remains of Pleasant Ridge United Church of Christ in the Pleasant Ridge Community of Guilford County during the early morning hours of Friday, June 28, 1996.

(AP Photo/News and Record, Nelson Kepley)

A fire engulfs a wooden sanctuary at the Matthews-Murkland Presbyterian church in Charlotte, N.C. as seen in this image taken off television Thursday night, June 6, 1996.

(AP Photo/NBC NEWS TODAY)

The National Council of Churches has established a Burned Churches Fund to rebuild Black churches. Above, an NCC delegation visits the site of the St. Paul's Primitive Baptist Church in Meridian, Mississippi.

(NCC Photo)

All that remains of the interior at Mt. Zion Baptist Church.

(Harvey Finkle)

A young member of the congregation helping to clean up Little Zion Baptist Church, Boligee, Alabama.

(Harvey Finkle)

The congregation returns to the
rebuilt Little Zion Baptist Church,
Boligee, Alabama.

(Harvey Finkle)

way a unity of heart and mind characteristic of those who share a faith in Christ (Acts 4:32–35). To put the matter another way, the sharing of possessions practiced by this original Christian community in Jerusalem is presented as more a sacramental than a moral act. Their decision to have all things in common was not undertaken, in the first instance, to fulfill a moral obligation but to provide for all to see "an outward and visible sign of an inward and spiritual grace."

This particular narrative suggests, therefore, that actions of the church which have their origin in its *koinonia* properly have a special motivation and intentionality that distinguish them from more general acts of benevolence. They are properly motivated by mutual love, and their intention is, in the first instance, to give expression to the unity of all believers in Christ. They are consequently, first and foremost a form of witness to the power of God that breaks down the barriers that divide the peoples and races of the earth. They are intended as external, sacramental expressions of a special sort of relationship. The Lukan narrative about sharing possessions suggests by analogy that Christians who supported the Burned Churches Project as an expression of their *communion* with the members of the burned-out houses of worship ought most properly to understand their actions as motivated by mutual love and intended to express and establish unity with those whose houses of worship were burned. Contrary to the most likely reaction of American Christians who may see a more expressly moral reason for their action, the actions of the Gentile churches to the distress of the poor in Jerusalem are better understood as a form of witness to the unity of all *believers* in Christ than as an expression of *solidarity* with *fellow citizens* who are in distress.

III

A similar conclusion about the way in which the Burned Churches Project is most properly understood from a Christian perspective is suggested by Paul's account of the collection for the poor in Jerusalem which he organized among the Gentile churches. This statement may at first seem strange because, unlike the sharing of goods in the original Jerusalem community, the collection for the Jerusalem church was so obviously designed with what would now be called a moral purpose in mind. Thus, in Paul's account of the Jerusalem Council, he notes that in extending the right hand of fellowship *(dexias . . . koinonias)*, James, Peter and John urged that Paul and Barnabas, along with the Gentile churches, "remember the poor" (Gal. 2:9–10). No doubt the poor Jewish Christians in Jerusalem needed help. It is reasonable, therefore, for a modern reader to conclude that the collection for the Jerusalem poor had a singularly moral purpose, namely, a perceived obligation to relieve the want among co-religionists. There are, however, insuperable problems with this, the most likely contemporary interpretation. First of all, it seems that many of the Gentile churches were as poor or poorer than their Jewish counterpart in Jerusalem (2 Cor. 8:2). It is at best odd to claim that co-religionists would assume a moral obligation to help their needy brothers and sisters in circumstances where their relief effort simply increased their own privation. Moreover, the fact that the collection had its inception in the midst of a dispute over the significance of circumcision and a decision on the part of Jewish Christians to extend the right hand of fellowship to those not circumcised makes a univocal moral interpretation of this relief effort even less convincing. It would appear that its purpose was not in the first instance to fulfill a moral obligation to co-religionists who are poor, but to give concrete expression to the newly initiated and at best fragile *koinonia* or communion in Christ between Jew and Greek.

Paul himself gives the collection this interpretation. In referring to the money to be collected, he does not speak directly of money but of grace *(charis)*, communion *(koinonia)*, ministry *(diakonia)*, church service *(liturgia)*, and blessing *(eulogia)*. As Lionell Thornton once remarked, "St. Paul, by his choice of words, was sometimes suggesting deliberately the connection of commonplace things (e.g., a collection for the poor) with the highest mysteries of the Gospel" (i.e., the unity of all believers in Christ regardless of their earthly distinctions).[4] Thus, Paul repeatedly refers to the collection of money as "this grace" *(charin*, 2 Cor. 8:6, 7; 9:19) and, in this context, he speaks of "the grace *(charin)* of God which has been given in the churches of Macedonia" (2 Cor. 8:1). His point was that the generosity of the Gentile churches in Macedonia gave concrete expression to the grace they had received in Christ—the same grace received by the Jewish believers with whom they now shared all the benefits of Christ's death and resurrection. Thus, the Macedonians (and Paul) view their sacrificial gift as imitative of Christ's sacrificial gift to them and so also expressive of the sacrificial giving that is one of the central marks of the church's communion. Or, to put the matter another way, the life of the church is comprised of a chain of sacrificial gifts which together constitute its *koinonia*. As Christ gives his life for the church, so those who believe in him give their lives and their possessions as a gift to God and to their brothers and sisters in Christ (2 Cor. 8:1–5).

Viewing the Burned Churches Project through the lens of this narrative, what, by analogy, does one see? The collection for the poor in Jerusalem suggests that as the Gentile churches felt (because of the fragility and importance of relations between Jewish and Gentile Christians) they were under a special obligation to give concrete expression to the communion and partnership they enjoyed with the Jewish church in Jerusalem, so also Christians and their churches in America are under a special obligation to show that racial divisions are not in any way properly a part of the definition of the *koinonia* of the church. As Paul gave special priority to the collection for the saints in Jerusalem because he wanted to make clear that the pervasive division between Jew and Greek ought in no way to compromise the communion of believers, so also support by Christians for the Burned Churches Project ought to be given priority among believers in America in order to show that the long history of racism in America ought in no way to compromise the common life of America's churches.

To put the matter more directly, even if we grant that relations between Jews and Christians have a special theological significance that is not present in this case, it is reasonable to say that, by analogical extension, the implication of the narrative for relations between African Americans and whites in America is as follows. In each time and place, there appear particular threats to the church's communion. More often than not these threats issue from differences in class, race, or nationality.

When these threats are present and Christians from one class, race, or nationality find themselves in need, Christians from whom those in need might be divided by these wrongful distinctions have a special obligation to undertake concrete forms of action that make clear that the divisions in question have no proper place in the definition of the Christian fellowship.

If this reading of Luke and Paul is correct and if these narratives have, by analogy, been used properly to illumine present circumstances, certain important conclusions follow. The first is that both white and black Christians in America have a special obligation to undertake expressive actions which make clear that race ought in no way to condition the church's communion. The second is that when harm is done to black Christians by whites they, the white Christians, have a particularly binding responsibility to come to the aid of their black brothers and sisters. This responsibility is generated by the nature of the gospel itself. It is a necessary witness to the unity of all believers in Christ.

There is a final conclusion suggested by Paul's collection for the poor. As has been pointed out, the narrative suggests a special obligation, generated by the central content of Christian belief, to come to the aid of those in need if there are sources of division between them and other Christians with whom they are in relation. The story, however, does not suggest that Christians have a general obligation in all circumstances to show favor to fellow believers. For example, this particular narrative in no obvious way lends support to something like the *Christian Yellow Pages*. It suggests no reason for always favoring co-religionists in business dealings, political relations or even charitable acts. The narrative in question seems to point only to a particular form of responsibility—a responsibility for fellow believers that comes into effect in instances when the co-religionists in question find themselves in need and are (a) people with whom one enjoys a history of relationship and (b) people from whom one might, for unacceptable reasons, be divided. The obligation for support comes into play first of all because the truth of the gospel and the nature of the church may be compromised if nothing is done. In such cases, believers have a duty to God and one another to make clear that the parties in question are bound by ties that transcend the barriers that might separate them and render them either strangers or enemies.

IV

The story of Peter's vision in which he is commanded to eat unclean food provides a further explanation of the importance of Paul's efforts on behalf of the *koinonia* of the church (Acts 10—11). It provides as well a theological frame of reference from within which the Burned Churches Project ought to be understood by Christians. Peter responds to the command by saying that he has never eaten anything "common." The Greek for common is *koinon,* a word obviously related to *koinonia.* By agreeing to eat what is common or impure *(koinon),* Peter declares that the fellowship *(koinonia)* of the church has no place for the ancient barriers of impurity, race, nationality, color, caste, or class. If any of these barriers to human unity come into play within the life of the church, the very nature not only of the church but also of the Christian gospel is compromised.

These observations make it reasonable to say that behind the Burned Churches Project properly lie a set of motives, intentions, and obligations which are unique to Christians and which differentiate the nature of their response to this particular set of circumstances from that of the general population. The circumstances that generated the Burned Churches Project are ones in which the Christian gospel itself has been compromised. For this reason, white American Christians may be said to have an obligation to their black brothers and sisters that is generated by the central tenets of Christian belief. As such, they have an obligation that binds them in a way that the demands of sympathy and benevolence do not bind the general public.

In sum, to the extent that the Burned Churches Project, like the collection for the poor in Jerusalem, is an expression of the *koinonia* of the church, because the history of relations between black and white Christians in America manifests such a failure of common life, certain motives, intentions, and obligations ought in a very strict sense to lie behind the project if it indeed is to be called an expression of *koinonia.* These motives, intentions and obligations, because they are expressive of a mutual relation in Christ, are necessarily distinct from those which may lie behind the actions of the general public. The distinctive motive is the mutual love that properly characterizes the communion of the church. The distinctive intention is to make a witness to the unity of all believers in Christ. The distinctive obligation is to make a witness to the unity of the church in circumstances where both the truth of the gospel and the common life of the church might otherwise be compromised.

V

A concluding set of remarks is necessary to demarcate the demands of *koinonia* that arise in circumstances like those which surround the collection for the saints and the Burned Churches Project from those that arise in circumstances that are relevantly different. The obligation present in these circumstances is strictly binding because the parties involved have been divided by unacceptable factors and they are required by the truth of the gospel itself to undertake actions which overcome these barriers to unity. What, however, is the case when, as in China today, Christians are being persecuted not by coreligionists but by people who both deny the existence of God and seek to prevent Christian worship of God? What actions, motives, and intentions, if any, are required of Christians in other parts of the world—Christians who do not have historical ties to those being persecuted? In what ways, if any, do they have obligations simply as co-religionists to come to the aid of their brothers and sisters? If, in circumstances like these, there are specifically Christian obligations implied by the *koinonia* of the church how stringent are they? Or, moving further afield, does the *koinonia* of the church imply any special obligations on the part of Christians if devotees of other religions are in some way being persecuted? Finally, if Christians, on account of the *koinonia* of the church, have special obligations of whatever sort, be they to co-religionists or to others, in what way are these obligations different from the obligations they may have to others simply as fellow citizens or fellow human beings?

It lies beyond the scope of this essay to attempt an answer to these pressing questions. To be sure, they are questions that are implied by the argument sketched above. Nevertheless, it is clear that one answer does not fit all cases when one is searching for the actions, motives, and intentions that are implied by the fact that Christians enjoy the sort of relation summed up in the term *koinonia*. If anything, this essay is meant to suggest that the implications of *koinonia* are complex and that different aspects of the Christian story may have to be brought into play to determine, as circumstances vary, exactly what those implications are. What is certain is that the burning of black churches, the persecution of Christians in China, and the attempts to eliminate Buddhism in Tibet each present Christians who live within the communion of saints with rather different issues and consequently rather different aspects of what it means to enjoy the grace of Christ, the love of God, the communion of the Holy Spirit.

The author would like to thank his colleague and friend Prof. Gene Outka of the Yale Divinity School for having read and commented on an earlier draft of this paper.

Notes

1. The Rev. Dr. Joan Brown Campbell, "The Burned Churches Project." Testimony before the U.S. House of Representatives' Committee on the Judiciary. March 19, 1997, p. 7.

2. Ibid.

3. My understanding of the full meaning of these passages has been aided in a significant way by the treatment they receive in L.S. Thornton's book *Common Life in the Body of Christ*. It remains, I believe, the single best treatment of *koinonia* as a way of construing the nature of the church. See L.S. Thornton, C.R., *Common Life in the Body of Christ*, (Westminster: Dacre Press, 1941).

4. Ibid., p. 27.

6

Ecumenical Solidarity

Emmanuel Clapsis

The National Council of the Churches of Christ in the USA (NCCC) has mobilized Christian churches, people of other living faiths, charitable organizations, and the government against racism and has offered support, material as well as spiritual, to those African American congregations whose houses of worship have been burned by racially motivated people. The outburst of such violent acts is a strong reminder that evil and its destructive forces, in this case racism, cannot be conquered in this life once and for all. At the same time it must not be forgotten that in this fragmented world God is actively present, through the Holy Spirit, working for the liberation of humanity and of the whole creation from the bondage of death and oppression.

The resurrection of Jesus Christ is the foundation of the Christian hope that ultimately the future belongs to God and that the whole creation is destined to participate in God's glory through its unity with and in Jesus Christ. Those who have accepted the Christian gospel and have been baptized in the name of the Holy Trinity are grafted onto Christ's body and willfully participate in God's mission for the salvation of the world. It is their responsibility through vigilance, discernment, and prayer to recognize the will of God in the midst of historical ambiguities and through acts of love to enhance the recognition of this presence so the world may believe and be saved.

The mobilization of churches through the NCCC initiative against racism and its oppressive outbursts must be understood as an *ecclesial act*. It provides an opportunity to the churches to communicate to the world, through concrete acts, what they have become as a result of their unity with Jesus Christ. The awareness of God's presence in their lives transforms faithful people and the churches of God into inexhaustible sources of love that bring life to the world. The second-century Athenian philosopher Aristides explains in his *Apology* the actions of Christians as a reflection of their faith in Jesus Christ:

> Christians trace their origin to the Lord Jesus Christ . . .
> They have the commandments of the Lord Jesus Christ Him-
> self impressed upon their hearts, and they observe them,
> awaiting the resurrection of the dead and the life of the world
> to come . . . They hasten to do good to their enemies. They
> are gentle and reasonable. They abstain from every unlawful
> exchange and from all uncleanness. They despise not the
> widow, nor do they distress the orphan. Whoever has, distrib-
> utes liberally to him [*sic*] that has not. Should they see a
> stranger, they take him under roof, and rejoice over him as
> over a blood brother. For not after flesh do they call them-
> selves brethren, but after the spirit. For the sake of Christ
> they are ready to lay down their lives.[1]

Through the NCCC's Burned Churches Project churches do not merely express their sadness for undesirable acts of violence by contributing, from a distance, monetary assistance toward the rebuilding of the churches. Rather, they express their deter-mination to be in solidarity with the victimized congregations, addressing the temporary but real wounds and losses that rac-ism has inflicted, helping them to restore their temples of wor-ship in order to continue their ministries of praising God and serving the world. By such a comprehensive pastoral and heal-ing approach, the churches have recognized that, while they need to address the immediate needs of these congregations, they must also sensitize the people of God that such demonic acts will continue as long as we do not recognize the evil and violence borne by racism. For the Christian churches in the United States, according to Joan Brown Campbell, NCCC Gen-eral Secretary, racism is "a spiritual issue—an evil—sin, acted out against God and the neighbor."[2] It is a social illness that prevents the recognition of the common humanity that all peo-ple share and participate in despite their irreducible differences.

Orthodoxy Against Racism

Orthodox churches, through the Standing Conference of Or-thodox Bishops in North America, are active participants and

, supporters of the efforts of the NCCC against racism and its violent outbursts. They are in solidarity with those congregations which have lost their houses of worship in fires fueled and ignited by racism. The Orthodox bishops in a common statement have expressed this solidarity between their churches and the victimized congregations:

> As leaders of the Orthodox Church we stand with those people who have suffered this devastation. We urge all of our faithful to join with us in assisting the rebuilding of these vandalized and desecrated houses of worship. We call upon all people to declare that bigotry, bias, and violence must be erased from society.[3]

The bishops considered the burning of black churches a serious assault on the basic principles of religious liberty and tolerance that characterize life in a free and democratic society. The houses of worship as living signs of the communion that people have with God and with each other are focal expressions of the love, hope, and freedom that God has bestowed so graciously upon his people. Those who ignited the fires desired to prevent African Americans from receiving these gifts of God which are so necessary for life. The bishops urged Christians under their jurisdiction to be in solidarity with the suffering African American congregations, helping them to reconstruct their temples of worship and actively to work against racism. Archbishop Iakovos, the former primate of the Greek Orthodox Archdiocese of North and South America, through an encyclical addressed to the faithful, not only condemned these heinous acts of racial violence but also communicated the meaning of Christian solidarity. He stated:

> God has created us as one family under his grace and benevolence. The experiences of one person or one group of persons are essentially embraced by all other members of our human family. In times of triumph and in times of defeat, in times of health and in times of illness, in times of natural disaster and in times of tragedy from human failures we must identify with one another.

Such is the reality of the current tragedy, which comes from human failure, or the arson burning of churches. Houses of worship constructed with the funds of believers who desire only to offer praise to God, to study his word and to fellowship with one another in service to others have been utterly destroyed. Good people's love and wholesome deeds have been desecrated.

We all must embrace their devastation. We all must shoulder their challenges. We all must join together in rebuilding their faith, in strengthening their resolve and in reconstructing their homes of worship.[4]

Orthodox theologians have also repudiated racism as a great sin against God's creation:

It is a great insult to the God-given dignity of human beings that various forms of discrimination on the basis of race, color, creed and culture are practiced in our world today . . . Christian faith affirms that diversity of race and culture reflects the beauty of God's creation. To deny the inherent right of people to affirm their identity with self-respect, dignity and openness to others is a sin against God's creation.[5]

In the same report the Orthodox theologians recognize that denouncing the problem of racism is not enough. The church must express its deep-rooted commitment to justice through concrete and relevant acts.

We must affirm, loudly and clearly, the truth that God's image is present in every human being. We need to seek out and actively cooperate with all forces of good working for the eradication from God's creation of all forms of prejudice and discrimination. We ourselves must teach our people to respect the integrity and dignity of all peoples of every nation, economic condition, race, sex, political affiliation, so that reconciliation and tolerance may replace coercion and violence in our relationships.[6]

The Orthodox churches, along with other Christian churches, have recognized that actions against racism and

solidarity with the victims of violence and oppression is a faithful response to God's loving presence in their midst.

Ecclesiology and Ethics

In the ecumenical movement it has never been disputed that
for the recovery of the visible unity of God's church, the divided
churches must not only recover their unity in faith, reach a common understanding of baptism and eucharist, and recognize
each others' ministries and structures of authority, but they
must also find ways to express together their unity through acts
of witness that reveal their participation in God's active love for
the world: "The Church is the community of people called by
God who, through the Holy Spirit, are united with Jesus Christ
and sent as his disciples to witness and to participate in God's
reconciliation, healing and transformation of creation."[7]

The existing unity of God's people is visibly expressed and
communicated to the world whenever and wherever the
churches, despite their differences, are able to contemplate together the presence and action of God in history and, based
on such common deliberation after due discernment, commit
themselves in actions that reflect their unity in Jesus Christ
and their commitment to participate in God's mission for the
salvation of the world. In the spirit of such an understanding,
the Faith and Order Movement at its Third World Conference in
Lund, Sweden, 1952, addressed the following challenge to the
churches: "should not our churches . . . act together in all matters except those in which deep differences of conviction compel
them to act separately?"[8] As the churches act in the world
through the transformative power of the gospel, they reveal their
already existing unity in Jesus Christ. This unity is an event,
an act of the Holy Spirit who binds them into *koinonia* despite
their apparent divisions in history. In the *koinonia* that churches
experience through their common *diakonia* to the world, they
become consciously aware of the fact that they belong to one
another despite differences. This discovery of common origins
and calling becomes the basis of their quest and commitment
to recover the visible unity of God's church in the common
confession of the apostolic faith, sacramental communion, reconciliation of ministries, and common witness to the world.

The great contribution of the modern ecumenical movement is the fact that churches through common deliberation have discovered the common mind of the church in such ethical matters as violence and racism. In these common deliberations concerning the church's presence in the modern world, they also have realized the depth and gravity of their disagreement on other ethical issues, particularly issues of sexuality such as homosexuality, abortion, and contraception. The churches have been drawn closer to each other, into a fuller sense of community, on the basis of the discovery of their shared ethical concerns even while ethical disagreements have accentuated their divisions. While "speaking the truth in charity" (Eph. 4:15) the churches are called as far as possible "to maintain the unity of the Spirit in the bond of peace" (Eph. 4:13) and to avoid wounding further the imperfect but real *koinonia* that the Spirit of God has given them through ecumenical fellowship. They have been able through ecumenical encounter to attain a significant convergence on at least some ethical principles and thus they have achieved a basic framework for further common ethical deliberation and action.

> While Christians, both individually and as churches do not always reach the same solutions to some of the ethical problems facing human communities, they have values, the values of the Kingdom, to guide them. These include for example: the sanctity of life; the dignity and equality of all human beings created in God's image and redeemed by Christ; the responsibility to create and develop patterns of life in which justice, peace and respect for all creation can flourish. These values have their origin in our understanding of God's love and express aspects of authentic communion between God and humanity.[9]

Churches, as they encounter the irreducible moral pluralism that exists within each particular community and as they reach common understanding of what God demands from them in concrete situations, are beginning to discover how important it is to develop guidelines on how they should conduct ecumenical dialogue in respect to moral issues. Such dialogue may not always lead to agreement, yet it is needed to maintain the sense of community even in the face of irreducible moral differences. The Joint Working Group between the Roman Catholic Church and the World Council of Churches has produced guidelines for ecumenical dialogue on ethical issues that provide a framework of conversation that maintains *koinonia* even in the face of potentially divisive moral questions. These guidelines provide helpful insight on how churches can understand each other's moral visions without compromising the integrity of their own positions. They specifically suggest:

1. In fostering *koinonia* or communion between the churches, we should as much as possible consult and exchange information with one another, in a spirit of mutual understanding and respect, always "speaking the truth in charity" (Eph. 4:15).

2. In dialogue we should try first to understand the moral positions and practices of others as they understand them, so that each one recognizes oneself in the descriptions. Only then can we evaluate them out of our own tradition and experience.

3. In comparing the good qualities and moral ideals or the weakness and practices of various Christian communities, one should compare ideals with ideals and practice with practice. We should understand what others want to be and to do in order to be faithful disciples of Christ, even though those others—as we ourselves—are burdened with weakness and sin.

4. We recognize that Christians enjoy a history of substantial unity in moral teaching and practice. By placing ethical issues within this inheritance of moral unity, we can more carefully understand the origin and nature of any present disagreement or division.

5. We trust that Christians can discover the bases for their moral vision, values and conduct in the Scripture and in other sources: moral tradition (including specific Church and inter-church statements), liturgies, preaching and catechetics, pastoral practices, common human experiences and methods of reflection.

6. We should seek from the empirical sciences the best available knowledge on specific issues, and if possible agree on

the data and their ethical implications before offering moral guidance.

7. We should acknowledge that various Church traditions in fact sometimes agree, sometimes differ in the ways they:

— use Scripture and other common resources, as well as the data of empirical sciences;

— relate moral vision, ethical norms and prudential judgments;

— identify a specific moral issue and formulate the problems;

— communicate within a Church those values and disciplines which help to develop its own moral environment in the shaping of Christian character;

— understand and exercise ministerial leadership and oversight in moral guidance.

8. We should be ever alert to affirm whatever is shared in common, and to admit where there are serious divergent, even contrary stances. We should never demand that fellow Christians with whom we disagree compromise their integrity and convictions.

9. In the public arena of pluralistic societies, we should be in dialogue also with others, whether religious or secular. We try to understand and evaluate their moral insights and judgments, and to find a common language to express our agreements and differences.

10. When the dialogue continues to reveal sincere but apparently irreconcilable moral positions, we affirm in faith that the fact of our belonging together in Christ is more fundamental than the fact of our moral differences. The deep desire to find an honest and faithful resolution of our disagreements is itself evidence that God continues to grace the *koinonia* among disciples of Christ.[10]

There is a need for the churches to deliberate on why their ethical judgments sometimes differ and whether or not such differences justify division or demand further conversation grounded in their God-given *koinonia*. In the process of such deliberation, churches may discover that the origins of their ethical discord are not differing understandings of the Christian faith, but rather differing interpretations of this faith in relation to concrete situations of life. Christians may differ with one another in ethical judgments because they understand differently—and with various degrees of comprehension—the complexities of life situations, and consequently sometimes choose to relate differentiated understandings of reality to different aspects of their common faith. Thus diversity of ethical response is an inevitable characteristic of the churches' witness to life situations in the modern world. The moral cohesiveness of the churches is safeguarded by the fact that their ethical responses to life situations are only applications of the gospel to those situations. Furthermore, since in today's world we recognize not only the historicity of the Christian faith but also that of our own beings, it is important for the churches to recognize *conversation* as an important instrument which advances the unity of the churches and limits the subjective and arbitrary interpretations not only of faith but also of social reality. The importance of such conversation becomes evident as we bear in mind that all Christians are united both in their intention to be in continuity with the apostolic faith found in Scripture and in their desire to see the world live through the coming reality of God's reign.

While there is agreement that common reflection and action on ethical matters advance the quest for the unity of the church, theologians continue to disagree on whether the church as "God's gracious gift to us" is so conditioned by ethics that "there is no ecclesiology without ethics and no ethics without ecclesiology." Such an affirmation confuses or rather identifies God's salvific presence in the world with the human response to God's invitations for a covenantal relationship. While the church as the body of Christ and the temple of the Holy Spirit is the active presence of God in the world, it is not always true that the collective and personal action of the faithful and of their communities, even with good intentions, express or are identical with God's will and action. A visible sign of the unity and identification of the faithful with God in the church's sacramental life is the moral transformation of their lives so that they can be signs of God's transformative presence in the world. "While the church is not constituted by or dependent for its ongoing existence upon the moral activities of its members, the holiness of the church calls for their constant moral struggle."[11] The concept of discipleship describes the personal and collective participation of Christians in the church's holiness. Of course, the complexities and ambiguities of history are such that in order to do the will of God, Christians and the church have the responsibility to discern, by the power of the Holy Spirit and on the basis both of the church's tradition and its eschatological expectations, the signs of the times (Matt. 16:1–4). This leads to the need to recognize the importance of connecting Christian ethics with the liturgy which is the act where the being of the church in relation to the fullness of creation is actualized and communicated. The 1982 Faith and Order statement on *Baptism, Eucharist and Ministry* (BEM) states:

> The Eucharist embraces all aspects of life. It is a representative act of thanksgiving and offering on behalf of the whole world. The eucharistic celebration demands reconciliation and sharing among all those regarded as brothers and sisters in the one family of God and is a constant challenge in the search for appropriate relationships in social, economic and political life (Matt. 5:23f.; 1 Cor. 10:16f; 1 Cor. 11:20–22; Gal. 3:28). All kinds of injustice, racism, separation and lack of freedom are radically challenged when we share in the body and blood of Christ.[12]

Orthodox theologians insist that through the eucharist we see and experience the world as God sees it and relates to it in its eschatological future. For this reason, the eucharistic experience of the world and the gospel of Jesus Christ become the foundation of the ethical principles that regulate the life of the church in history.[13] These ethical principles cannot in themselves guarantee the presence of the *eschaton* in history since the coming reign of God, as an unconditional gift of God to the world, remains the ultimate criterion for judging whether or not ideas or actions in this world are expressions of the eschatological future. This should not produce indifference to ethics and history but must rather be the basis of the church's involvement in the life of the world through ethical action that embraces the totality of life without pretending that such actions exhaust the gospel or that the coming reign of God somehow depends on or is conditioned by human actions.

Ecumenical Solidarity

Theologically, how should we understand the ecumenical fellowship and concern that churches manifest as they assist other Christian churches in need? The overwhelming response of churches to the initiative of the NCCC in assisting African American congregations to rebuild their houses of worship could be seen merely as an occasion for churches and others to express their good will and compassion. This, of course, is the way that some have understood and participated in this effort. Theologically, however, we must insist that in such acts of solidarity the being of the church is revealed and communicated. *Diakonia* to those in need is an overflowing of God's grace that enables the people of God to be in *koinonia* with one another and moves them to an even greater *koinonia* with the totality of the world. Thus, in acts of *diakonia* those who benefit from the manifestation of the plenitude of God's grace are not only those who are in need of assistance but also those who offer such assistance and support. In the acts both of giving and receiving, people and communities become conscious of their unique identity, an identity that reflects their unity with God.

The *diakonia* of the churches cannot be understood apart from the *koinonia* that they already share in their unity in Jesus Christ. The Fifth World Conference on Faith and Order, 1993, affirmed communion with Christ and one another in God's church as entailing, among many other things, "a sense of justice and compassion; a sharing in one another's joys, sorrows and sufferings (2 Cor. 1:6–7; Heb. 10:33; et al.); . . . serving one another in love and mutual receiving and giving material and spiritual gifts (Rom. 15:26–27; 2 Cor. 8:1–15; Gal. 5:13)."[14] Churches without *diakonia*—in the sense of service, solidarity, and active assistance to those in need—do not have at their disposal the language needed to communicate to the world what it is that is taking place in their own inner lives. *Diakonia* reveals to the world what the church is by the grace of God. It is the overflowing of God's grace to the totality of creation. If all the churches participate in God's mission for the salvation of the world, through their unity by the power of the Holy Spirit in Jesus Christ, what does their *diakonia* to the world imply about their relation to one another?

In this context we must explore the ecclesiological significance of inter-church *diakonia* for the advancement of the church's unity. Inter-church *diakonia* enables the local churches to liberate themselves from all forms of self-sufficiency. It empowers the churches to recognize that despite their differences they are in unity with one another through the work of the Holy Spirit, joint participants in God's trinitarian life and love. It is because of this transcendent unity that the particular churches cannot experience the catholicity of the church's life unless they are co-responsible to one another for the fullness of the faith, receive one another's gifts, learn from each other's experiences, and share in each other's sufferings. For one local church to give material or spiritual aid—even material or spiritual existence—to another, means that it is a church which shares in fellowship the one grace of God, fulfilled in Christ and by the power of the Holy Spirit. The church of God, through *diakonia* among the particular churches, reflects trinitarian life on earth as an indivisible communion of saints throughout the whole world. What a particular church becomes through her vertical relationship with God needs to be expressed in her horizontal unity, through *diakonia,* with all other particular churches so that their *koinonia* in service will reveal the wholeness of God's church. This kind of unity is a credible sign to the world of God's transformative love that brings all into unity without obliterating the richness of human diversity.

The particular churches perpetuate the division of God's church and compromise its catholicity whenever they perceive their *diakonia* to the world as a unilateral duty to be carried on by each one of them separately with no sense of interdependence. Local churches absorbed by the immediacy of their own situations become comfortable in their isolation from the rest of the Christian churches. Anxiety to address the needs of such limited environments demonstrates a lack of concern for the *diakonia* of God's church to the whole world and is, in fact, a demonstration of the self-sufficiency that plagues the lives of local congregations. The way that a particular church serves the world may enhance and perpetuate the division of the church if the local church persists in acting independently of other particular churches. *Diakonia* in *koinonia* with the fullness of God's church, the communion of all local churches, reveals an already existing unity with Jesus Christ through the Holy Spirit. It helps the communion of churches to empower and actualize the ministry of the whole church to the whole world through the fullness of the gifts that the Holy Spirit has bestowed on all, leading them from unity in *diakonia* to unity in faith, life, and confession. The unity of God's church is enhanced and revealed to the world whenever local churches act in unity with one another, witnessing to the presence of God in the world.

Notes

1. Aristides of Athens, *Apologia pro religione Christiana.*

2. Joan Brown Campbell, Testimony to the Committee on the Judiciary, U.S. House of Representatives, March 19, 1997.

3. Statement of the Standing Conference of Canonical Bishops (SCOBA) Condemning the Desecration and Burning of Churches in the United States, June 21, 1996.

4. Encyclical to the Hierarchs, the Reverend Clergy, the Parish Councils of the Greek Orthodox Parishes, the Philoptochos Societies and the Youth of the Holy Archdiocese of North and South America, Protocol No. 19, June 18, 1996.

5. Gennadios Limouris, ed., *Justice, Peace and the Integrity of Creation: Insights from Orthodoxy* (Geneva: World Council of Churches, 1990), p. 7.

6. Ibid., p. 13.

7. Thomas F. Best and Gunther Gassman, eds. *On the Way to Fuller Koinonia: Official Report of the Fifth World Conference on Faith and Order,* Faith and Order Paper No. 166 (Geneva: World Council of Churches, 1994), p. 259 (Report of Group IV, para. 25).

8. Oliver S. Tomkins, ed., *Faith and Order: The Report of the Third World Conference at Lund, Sweden: August 15–28, 1952,* Faith and Order Paper No. 15 (London: SCM Press, 1953), pp. 5–6.

9. Best and Gassman, op. cit., p. 291.

10. "The Ecumenical Dialogue on Moral Issues: Potential Source of Common Witness or of Divisions: A Study Document of the *Joint Working Group,*" *Ecumenical Review,* Vol. 48, No. 2 (April 1996), p. 154.

11. Thomas F. Best and Martin Robra, eds., *Ecclesiology and Ethics: Costly Commitment* (Geneva: World Council of Churches, 1995), p. 65.

12. *Baptism, Eucharist, and Ministry* (Geneva: World Council of Churches, Faith and Order Paper No. 111, 1982), p. 14, para. 20.

13. Emmanuel Clapsis, "Ecclesiology and Ethics: Reflections by an Orthodox Theologian," in Best and Robra, op. cit., pp. 28–42.

14. Best and Gassmann, op. cit., p. 274.

7

Through the Fire
A Theological Response to Burning Black Churches
James H. Evans, Jr.

Beginning in 1995 a series of fires destroyed or damaged African American churches, largely throughout the southern half of the United States; over the next two years more than 125 churches were set ablaze. From the outset these events set off national soul-searching. They have provided an opportunity for religious, civic, and political groups to examine their abilities to understand and respond to the crisis. What did these fires mean? Why were black churches the primary target? At a deep level, clearly, they were ignited by smoldering animosities and the embers of enmity which neither high democratic ideals nor religious tolerance could extinguish.

Individual Christian denominations responded by establishing funds to rebuild the churches. The National Council of the Churches of Christ in the USA coordinated a massive effort to collect and distribute monies for rebuilding. These efforts along with the contributions of numerous individuals and civic organizations were an impressive outpouring of Christian sympathy. Yet in spite of the charitable response of religious institutions, it remains difficult to escape the suspicion that the sentiments which either gave rise to or provided legitimization for these attacks—the burnings—remain deeply woven into the fabric of our society. They thus provide an occasion for reflection on the relation between what appear to be social problems and our most profound religious and theological beliefs. The burning of these black churches can be understood as a sign of our times, and they can also be understood as the most recent manifestation of a social malignancy which has perennially escaped both diagnosis and cure. They are a symbol of the loss of reverence for religious institutions and the authority which they represent, as well as a symbol of social anxiety brought on by a need for genuine spiritual renewal.

In this brief reflection, I want to suggest that there are three challenges which these events present to Christian communities in the U.S. today. What do these events say to our society about the policies which undergird the existence of racial hatred, the practices which sustain the dream of cultural supremacy, and the principles which shape programs of religious persecution? It is my contention that these events can only be adequately understood as the result of the confluence of racism, the quest for cultural supremacy and purity, and religious persecution.

Racial Hatred and Public Policy

Since the point of its origin, this nation has had to wrestle with the dilemma of the presence of people of color. The issue of race has been a singular lens through which the ideals which have collectively come to be called "The American Dream" have been refracted. American society has thus fashioned the rules which guide political life against the backdrop of race.

The burning of black churches in the last decade of the twentieth century, at first glance, appears to be unrelated to the burning and bombing of black churches during the 1950s and 60s. The significant progress made in the condition of some segments of the African American community would seem to suggest that the growth of racism has been stunted in our society. Rather than looking to racism as the motive for the burning of these churches, it might seem to make more sense to see these events as simply part of the violent times in which we live.

In a highly publicized action, the Christian Coalition, a group which has not historically been an advocate of the causes espoused by most African Americans, announced that they "would join forces with black Christians to stem the wave of suspicious fires sweeping black churches in the South and to help the affected congregations raise money to rebuild" (*The Washington Post*, June 19, 1996). This would suggest that racism should not be seen as the primary factor in this crisis. The fact that some of the burnings appeared to be the work of vandals who also victimized other houses of worship lent credibility to the initial conclusion that one could not establish links between the fires. *The Washington Post* in the same article reported that although the perpetrators of the fires "are generally white, male and young, usually economically marginalized or poorly educated, frequently drunk or high on drugs, [they are] rarely affiliated with hate groups, but often deeply driven by racism . . . Little evidence has emerged to suggest a national or regional conspiracy . . ." The point is often that racism is reduced to personal prejudice and, in this view, cannot be the foundation for the burning of the churches. However, Noah Chandler of the Center for Democratic Renewal has tellingly noted that "the conspiracy is race itself."

I would argue that the burnings of these black churches are acts of senseless violence which characterize the times in which we live. However, it is important to note that *while they are acts of senseless violence, they are are not acts of random violence.* All acts of racist terror are essentially *senseless* because their logic is inchoate and often hidden in the broad constellation of decisions which are made by governments, religious communities, corporations, financial institutions, and universities, as well as of those decisions made by families and individuals. This constellation of decisions is what is normally referred to as *policy.*

Public policy is normally understood to be a course of action defined by government or "whatever government chooses to do or not to do," as Thomas E. McCollough wrote in *The Moral Imagination and Public Life.* But policy can mean, more broadly, and as also discussed by McCullough with reference to David Easton, "the authoritative allocation of values for the whole society." For more than two hundred years in this society institutionalized racism was public policy. The policies of segregation and discrimination were based on values which were affirmed both at the level of major institutions and at the level of families and individuals. Even when the policies are no longer legally enforced, the moral infrastructure which initially gave them legitimacy may survive. This moral infrastructure which has supported racist policies in this society, moreover, has yet to be dismantled. Thus it is that racist policies, often in new and ingenious guises, are likely to reappear. This is the link

between the systematic dismantling of affirmative action policies and the apparently *senseless* burning of black churches.
Until we recognize that these burnings are not simply the acts
of individuals with racist tendencies, but are linked with the
morality which supports present and past policies, we will find
ourselves at a loss to explain their deeper significance.

Cultural Supremacy and Social Practices

In recent years the topic of cultural diversity has become
central in many discussions regarding the direction of the American society. Indeed, the presence and ascendancy of various
ethnic groups has presented significant challenges to what some
believe to be the "American way of life." Although the current
presentation of these concerns deserves attention in its own
right, it should not be forgotten that the basic paradigm for
these concerns was set as the nation struggled in the nineteenth
century with the question of the place of newly freed, and no
longer economically necessary, slaves.

The basic question was a simple one: having spent their
blood, sweat, and tears in the service of this nation, are these
Africans now as American as any other resident group or are
they not deserving of such acceptance? Towering figures such
as Frederick Douglass argued in the affirmative. Yet, given the
terrible circumstances of their forced removal from Africa, their
equally forced labor in a strange land, and the nearly genocidal
campaign against all of their sustaining institutions, were these
Africans not better off back in Africa or in some other land where
self-government was a possibility? Persons such as Martin R.
Delaney and others argued that this was the only viable option.
These two questions framed the famous "Emigration Debate"
of the nineteenth century. In the context of the present reflection, these questions were and still are at the heart of the controversy concerning cultural diversity. In essence, however, *the
issue is not about cultural diversity but about cultural supremacy.* The issue is not the accommodation of different cultural styles, but rather which culture would establish the norms
in those areas of social life deemed most important.

At the same time that this debate concerning the emigration
of black people was at its height, the Ku Klux Klan was estab-

lished. In 1866 in Pulaski, Tennessee, a group of former Confederate soldiers formed an organization to which they gave that name. Although the group was not formed to be a racist hate group, but a source of amusement for its members, it soon adopted a new and sinister mission: to commit acts of terror against newly freed slaves as well as blacks who had been free for some time. The copious literature on groups like the Klan has normally described them as racial supremacists, but it is important to note that their overall function has been to establish, guard, and reinforce a broad *cultural* supremacy. Certain values and affirmations were seen to be consistent with "the American way of life"; others were not so favored. While racial hatred has almost always been at the heart of these groups' raison d'etre, racial hatred is distinguished from cultural supremacy in that the latter establishes a response to its own racial hatred and prides itself on its internal organization and logic. Thus it is that many of these groups are now paramilitary organizations which pride themselves on their ability to collect "intelligence" concerning the secret activities of their selected enemies.

In large part, racial hatred establishes a cultural supremacy through the reinforcement of certain social practices. By cultural supremacy, I mean the elevation of the norms and mores of one culture over another, often by the use of force or intimidation. The purpose of this elevation is to counteract the alleged chaos and confusion which reigns when many cultural options are allowed to compete in the public square. A social practice is, according to Alasdair MacIntyre, a kind of human behavior which is complex, rooted in some history, and social insofar as it involves groups of people rather than individuals. The "American Way of Life" represents a set of practices which falls into this category. It may be understood as complex in that it involves a number of items, such as the affirmation of the rights of the individual, freedom, a quasi-religious foundation for government and society, etc. It is rooted in a history in which the valor of many generations of patriots who gave their lives for the American idea form the main pillars. It is social in that the preservation of this way of life is left in the hands of "the people" rather than in those of powerful individuals. This is why the idea of democracy is so basic to the American way of life.

Nevertheless, the presence of people of African descent continues to present a challenge to those social practices which comprise the ideal of the American way of life. The continuous thread of racism suggests that the social practices which define our society are not as complex as they would first appear. The blatant expunging of the stories of people of color from our national history makes this history invalid if it does not include the contributions of African Americans. The fact that many of the social practices which define the American way of life, such as voting, have not been marked by the participation of black people suggests that these practices are not truly social.

Black churches have historically provided a challenge to truncated notions of the American way of life. They have also provided an alternative modality of life for African Americans. It is quite possible that the mere presence and activism of black churches may, in the minds of some, symbolize unacceptable social practice. It will be difficult, if not impossible, fully to understand the burning of black churches unless they are seen within the context of the broad range of social practices which define our way of life.

Religious Persecution and Theological Principles

If there is one religious principle which has been at the center of modern American democracy it is that of *religious tolerance*. Roger Williams brought the notion of religious freedom as espoused by the Baptists to the American colonies. The principle of religious tolerance, in consequence, found its way into the major documents which define American society. The essence of this principle is that each person is entitled to practice his or her religion, or even no religion, as he or she desires. In this context it would appear that the specter of religious persecution from which many of the early American settlers fled, would have no place in our society.

The burnings of black churches in the South is, however, not to be understood only as acts of racial terror. They are, at heart, acts of religious persecution. In 1997 a number of churches in Northern Ireland, including a Baptist church, were set ablaze. The fires were purportedly set by Protestants in order to incite anti-Catholic sentiments within the ongoing religious conflict in Northern Ireland between Protestants and Catholics. There have, similarly, been instances in the United States where the burning of black churches has been "justified" by right-wing groups because the firebombing by government forces of the Branch Davidian cult compound in Waco, Texas, was allegedly an act of religious persecution. The image of the burning church is a powerful symbol of religious persecution.

Religious persecution appears to be as old as religion itself. In the first three centuries of the common era, Christians were persecuted by the Roman Empire as enemies of the state. Not only was their very presence perceived to be a threat to the established order, they were also seen as the source of the major disasters which befell the Empire. They were also accused of "hostility to the human race," *odium generis human,* and of practicing a "perverse religion," *prava religio.* Because these Christians were different they were assumed to be incapable of sustaining healthy moral traditions; they were often accused of incest, cannibalism, and atheism. On February 23, 303, the Emperor Diocletian issued an edict which brought the simmering persecution of the Christian community to a climax. That edict ordered the surrender and burning of all copies of the Christian Scriptures and the destruction of all churches.

During the Protestant Reformation, some thirteen centuries later, religious persecution again appeared even in the pursuit of religious freedom. Henry VIII burned Protestants at the stake as did Mary Tudor. John Calvin ordered Servetus, one of his opponents, to be burned in 1541. The destruction of places of worship, as well as the punishment of opposition leaders, was a consistent part of the program of religious persecution. Nevertheless, a common but often overlooked factor in religious persecution has been that it usually appears as the final result of a complex network of economic, social, political, and legal shifts and upheavals.

A pattern similar to this can be noted in the history of the African American church during the period of slavery. As slave Christians sought to gather for worship, they were often subjected to persecution. They were legally forbidden to gather in groups for any purpose. Andrew Bryan and George Liele, pastors of the first African Baptist Church in South Carolina were subjected to beatings for daring to convene African slaves for worship. Like the first-century Christians, slave Christians were forced to meet in secret under the threat of flogging or even death. Those who were caught were often whipped, maimed, lynched, and their bodies burned.

During the civil rights movement, a movement largely rooted in the African American church, several black churches were the targets of bomb attacks and burnings. In many cases the major salvific symbol of the Christian faith, the cross, was set ablaze as a particularly ironic symbol of terror.

The burning of black churches in the waning years of the twentieth century must be seen in relation to a history of religious persecution which seems to persist in human behavior, even in an era such as our own when superficial judgments suggest that we live in secular/agnostic times. The first century Christian church, the heretical churches of the Protestant Reformation (most often those of the "Radical Reformation"), and the African American church have a place in this history of persecution in common. In spite of the burning of their Bibles, their buildings, and their bodies, however, they have persevered. Religious persecution continues to take on new and sophisticated forms. It is tempting to see the burning of the black churches as simply an anomaly in the story of our progress toward an open society. In reality, however, one need not be a pessimist— just a realist—to see that this seemingly unconnected series of events, part of the long story of religious persecution, draws us toward the need for spiritual renewal.

Conclusion

The response of many religious organizations to the burning of black churches in the American South has been significant. Large amounts of money have been raised and spent to rebuild these houses of worship. Yet the question remains whether out of the ashes of our incinerated relationships we can find the strength and commitment to build stronger ties among the churches. The centrifugal forces caused by the struggles and challenges of survival make it increasingly difficult for churches to attend to forging the ties between them, ties which are so important to our understanding of what it means to be the church.

The burning of black churches must be understood within the context of the racism in the policies, practices, and principles which shape our society. The cure for our condition is not, however, the formation of new policies, practices, and principles. In the midst of social, political, and economic malaise what is needed is *spiritual renewal*. Such renewal cannot come about apart from attention to the entire complex of forces which form the crucible of our faith. Perhaps out of the charred remains of these places where "the least among us" sought God's nurture, we might ignite a new witness for Christ in the world.

8

"Sharing the Fire"
The Question of Advocacy
Deborah Flemister Mullen

This essay presumes that the reign of God is a reality of loving community in which all creatures created by God are welcomed to dwell together as beloved members of God's *oikos* or *kindom*. As an image for human community, it is an ideal existence in which every person is a child of God to be treated with dignity and respect. As an ethic, freedom, love, justice, mutuality, and reciprocity are core values in all relationships. As a movement, it is dynamic, all-encompassing and likely always to remain just beyond the reach of what is achievable for the church, the body of Christ.

As a vision, further, this reign of God is a path by which people of God find order in the midst of chaos and invest life with meaning. As a source of hope, it provides the capacity to believe in the evidence of things unseen (Heb. 11), especially in times of great trial and crisis. In the vernacular of the African American church, it is the sign of the inexplicable assurance that whatever the trouble, God is able to fix it and that no matter how bleak the outlook, God will "make a way out of no way!"

To be sure, the reign of God may hold different meanings for others. The point here is not to persuade anyone of its usefulness as a metaphor for relational faith in which God is always a real presence in the life of the believer. Rather, I start here because in my own attempts to "make sense" out of senseless hate crimes and racially motivated violence, I must begin with the promise which sustains me and in which I find renewed hope: that as God gave Noah the rainbow sign, I pray that for me and my household, *the rainbow is truly enough.*

When wounded, the body of Christ responds out of its "double-consciousness," as human community and as sign of God's kindom come on earth. Instead of responding to pain and suffering with attitudes and actions of recrimination, revenge, or retribution, the church takes up its mission of reconciliation armed with God's passion for love and justice and accompanied by the Holy Spirit, the Advocate, that distinctive presence of God which equips and sustains the church for its mission and ministry. This way of behaving in a crisis, forgoing acrimony and villainous assaults on those who perpetrate violence, is in contrast to the way of the world. It is the calling, the *vocatio* of the church whose life is bound to the faithful witness of Jesus Christ whose own life was lived as an enduring testimony to the power and truth of customs other than those which the world often dictates. Simply put, the church is called to follow the fidelity to God which Jesus himself modeled in the world. Easier said than done! Mission impossible? For sure, especially when all hell is breaking loose . . .

In contemporary American society, the church is a complicated company of Christians linked together in loose associations of voluntary membership organizations and separate communions. The distinctions between church bodies—shaped by historical and socio/cultural factors such as: ethnic/national origin (European vs. American-born); class/gender/race/sexual identity distinctions (affluent, poor, WomenChurch, black, Hispanic, white, Lesbigay, etc.); traditions of believing and behaving (Evangelical, Pentecostal, Roman Catholic, etc.)—have managed to keep them separated in both healthy and unhealthy ways. This essay claims that in matters related to race, by and large, the church has ceded its power to the demons instead of to the angels. The church has been unfaithful to its calling to follow Jesus for whom such distinctions as race, class, gender, etc., magnified the beauty and breadth of God's kingdom rather than deepened the reality of separation and division among God's people. *This unholy treason is not acceptable!* It is not acceptable particularly to those to whom the reality of God is sovereign and whose relationship with Jesus Christ stands as a public witness, even against a church identified with the "powers and principalities" of division and separation.

This essay, furthermore, boldly expresses hope in our human community's ability to achieve greater unity in spite of the diversity of our religious affiliations, or lack of such affiliation, and it expresses hope also in the ongoing public calling of the church to be both a catalyst in the movement for social justice and an agent of transformation in the world. Unapologetically, we believe that *the ecumenical church in North America ought to continue its critical public role* as "the repairer of the breach, the restorer of streets to live in" (Is. 58:12b). And finally, this essay affords its readers an opportunity to seize the present moment as an occasion to reflect on the good that can come from evil; by sharing lessons of good and of healing we testify, as the church arises *out of the ashes,* to the power of God to do a new thing, even in the face of increasing evidence that the social and spiritual cancer of racism threatens our whole body.

Public Witness . . . When the Rainbow is Enuf!

And here we are, at the center of the arc, trapped in the gaudiest, most valuable, and most improbable water wheel the world has ever seen. Everything now, we must assume, is in our hands; we have no right to assume otherwise. If we—and now I mean the relatively conscious whites and the relatively conscious blacks, who must, like lovers, insist on, or create, the consciousness of the others—do not falter in our duty now, we may be able, handful that we are, to end the racial nightmare, and achieve our country, and change the history of the world. If we do not now dare everything, the fulfillment of that prophecy, re-created from the Bible in song by a slave, is upon us: *God gave Noah the rainbow sign, No more water, the fire next time!*[1]

No more! . . . No more fires! No more lies! No more silence! This time it is too much, and the word is *No More!* This time the assault must be answered. There has been a response: individuals, faith communities, foundations, and denominational families acting together in a concerned effort to witness to the reality of civic responsibility and ecumenical unity have said, "Stop it, enuf, *No more!*"

No more! . . . to terrorism within the body of Christ, to midnight raids on the church buildings of unsuspecting sisters and brothers, largely located in isolated, rural areas of the South, often in economically vulnerable communities, with little or no insurance and cut off from emergency and municipal services. No more! . . . to the burning of African American houses of worship. No more to silence in the face of thinly veiled attempts to strike at the heart of the black community by burning its churches in a series of "seemingly" unrelated, questionably "random" acts of domestic terrorism. No more to the denial of patterns of racist motivation in a striking number of these church burnings. No more will the fires be overlooked or allowed to continue unexamined, covered up, or dismissed by the collective (un)consciousness of an America infected by racism's deadly virus. No more will the dividing of Christ's body be accepted by churches which confess the same Lord and yet remain indifferent to the racism within their own memberships.

The nation has been called to stop the burning and to take its witness against racial violence into the public arena. The rebuilding of African American church buildings has been assured, owing largely to the boldness, vigilance, and relentless pursuit of justice by the oldest and largest ecumenical organization in the country. Standing with the survivors of the devastated black churches in the ashes of *the fire this time,* the National Council of Churches is leading the resistance by marshalling the financial support of interreligious partnerships, private funding sources, the investigative and judicial powers of government, and by deploying a contingent of seasoned staff and volunteers to serve notice that the power of faith is still stronger than the power of evil. *This time* the fires set the terms, but no more . . . And, why should they *when the rainbow is enuf?* Or is it?

Divided by class, gender, nationality, race, and religion from our inception, we as American people have been and are engaged in a formidable struggle for the unity of the nation and the integrity of its soul. In this struggle, public and religious life have often danced the dance of mismatched partners: forever and unequally yoked, always "separated" by prohibitions intended at their creation to guarantee the liberty of citizens to practice their faith without recrimination *or* to abstain from religious affiliation without the threat of government or judicial interference. Throughout our history "individual rights" has been the rallying cry and a fitting motto for the heterogeneity and collective independent spirit of Americans. This "individualism" has set the pace for patterns of socialization in both the sacred and secular realms—how we marry, vote, worship, invest our money, and whether or not we respond to the plight of fellow citizens in need.

These facts of our American life together lead directly to the conclusion that while it is not unheard of in our nation to acknowledge and sometimes corporately to denounce and publicly grieve the painful realities of our dividedness—"one nation under God"?—it is now utterly unacceptable to glory in our gory past of racial division. We can no longer consign the future of our society to racial and class division. We can no longer retreat into cocoons of accepted yet tepid involvement *or* indifference when hate crimes, racial violence, or even the torching of church buildings rise up.

From the beginning there has been in this nation an uneasy peace between religious organizations and governmental agencies. At no time, however, has the intent been simply to prohibit the churches from exercising their right to public witness on matters of national concern or in times of crisis. To be sure, the churches have always played an important public role in our democratic society, especially by giving public support to order, freedom, and justice. Given the potential power of public witness, what the churches must now do is to act collectively by affirming that in instances when the human spirit is under siege and human life endangered, and when society as such can no longer protect (if it ever could) those who are the lost, the least, and the most vulnerable from injustice, there can be no hiding behind the lines demarcating church and state. In the case of the burned churches the line has been crossed! The church, ecumenically and as different communions, has both a moral and civic mandate to hold the public, including the representatives of government, accountable and to expect action "lest our feet stray from the places, our God, where we met thee" ("Lift Ev'ry Voice and Sing").

Indeed, James Baldwin was right: the circumstances around us are most bizarre. We are all participants, either in our salvation or our drowning. Baldwin remains, sadly, an undercelebrated giant and high priest of American "secul-ecclesio" criticism: "everything now, we must assume, is in our hands." To this we can only add our conviction that, grounded in the possibility of faith to transform things, we are made bold by God's power to redeem, rebuild, and restore. By that power, deployed to address injustice anywhere and everywhere, "we may be able, handful that we are, to end the racial nightmare, and achieve our country, and change the history of the world."

More than thirty years after Baldwin wrote, the people of America find themselves still very much on the cusp of a kind of *social anarchy* in which race matters for all the wrong reasons, in which race has become an excuse for all manner of mean-spirited and evil doings between individuals and groups. Our country's failure to put an end to racial discrimination and to acknowledge the pernicious nature and effects of white racism speaks eloquently to the absence of any moral authority in society credible enough to take up the "root causes" of racially determined social, class, and economic division. Our leaders in both church and society have largely failed to provide either the public rhetoric or the strategic plans required to break down the wrongly placed "walls of separation" behind which the "stinking thinking" of lynch mobs, red-lining financial institutions, everyday bigots, and, yes, church-burning arsonists cause evil to fester and triumph.

The church, which is itself a part of society, is, ironically, often implicated as part of the racial problem. The blending of secularity and religion in the church has often resulted in the "sacro-babble" of irrelevant pronouncements and ineffectual actions with respect to racial justice. Sometimes, though, an alliance of forces in church and society has been able to address common concerns in a way which has produced sustained progress in overcoming the brokenness and fragmentation which persistently threaten to destroy common impulses for unity. A case in point: the civil rights movement which, for all of its shortcomings, stands in recent history as a working model for effective public witness by the churches in respect to the struggle for equal rights for all Americans.

There is reason, then, not to lose hope that the church will stretch beyond its tendency simply to mimic its economic, political, and social surroundings in order to find a voice to resist compromise, including that of silence, in the face of the evil of racism. Temptations to cynical judgments about the irrelevance of the churches or their ineffectiveness as agents of racial reconciliation—11:00 A.M. on Sundays is *still* the most segregated hour in America—must not be allowed in any way to justify giving up on the power of the church's public witness to be *socially transforming* when enacted *ecumenically*. This witness always has the potential of being a vital force in the building up of renewed and transformed relationships between churches of different traditions and across the great divide of black and white.

As we continue to reflect on the burning of black churches, with some degree of critical distance between ourselves and events that have forever changed the quality of many persons' lives, perhaps we will be better able to discern what clues and questions have arisen from the ashes in respect both to the role of public witness and advocacy by the ecumenical church and to the impact of ecumenical solidarity between the churches. There may be a clue as well as a word of hope to be found in comments like those of Charles Reagan Wilson: "The arson of black churches can be seen as reflecting the same old racial tensions as in the past, but the reactions to the burnings raises a new question: Does the white response to the fires represent a moment of epiphany in black-white Christian relations in the South?" ("Church Burnings and Christian Community," *The Christian Century,* September/October, 1996).

While Professor Wilson may well be onto something of importance and worthy of attention over time, the more pressing question remains, for others, whether the high price paid by African Americans *once again* can be justified for any purpose, even that of helping white Christians in the South (or anywhere) finally to "get it." In light of the historical reality of racial relations during the first 400 years of American history, this latter question suggests that there can never be a "pay back" for the irretrievable price that racism has forced the black community to pay.

The Rev. Willie Barrow, chairperson of the Board of Directors of the Rainbow/PUSH Coalition, in her official statement expressing that organization's outrage over the destruction of African American churches, has offered yet another clue for our consideration. She wrote, "The burning of the Black Churches is an attempt to destroy the heart, soul and mind of the Black community. We are appalled at the destruction of our churches. However, make no mistake about it: Burning the buildings cannot destroy the Black Church, which resides in the soul of the people . . . Thank God that destroying the buildings cannot even singe the liberation power of the Black Church."[2] And in another statement, Bishop John Hurst Adams, Senior Bishop of the African Methodist Episcopal Church, called the leadership of the nation to task in no uncertain terms: ". . . we have a leadership-created climate that is mean, nasty and hateful. We have an erosion of faith and fear of God, with its downside enhanced by so many conflicting religious views . . . The official leadership at national, state, county and local levels must intentionally build a new climate of inclusion, quality and morality."[3]

When we can find some common ground on which to stand and decide together, we have the beginnings of an agenda for public witness by the church. This time, ironically, our first clues are to be found in the aftermath and charred rubble of African American houses of worship. The wanton arson of these buildings, representing a climate of escalating white racism and violence directed at African Americans because they are *black* Americans, has triggered a social, economic, political, and religious crisis in our nation. The African American community was, of course, quick to respond. Grassroots initiatives sprouted up, grew, and were buttressed in time by the attention paid to the fires by local councils of churches, national denominations, civil rights and voluntary organizations, the media, government agencies, and President Clinton himself. Thanks in large part to the public witness of the *ecumenical church*, particularly the aggressive and targeted action of the National Council of Churches, the whole world watched to see what America's total response would be to the desecration of African American sacred spaces caused by *the fire this time.*

The Ecumenical Church . . . The Unity of the Church as Koinonia, Gift and Calling

The purpose of God according to holy scripture is to gather the whole creation under the Lordship of Christ Jesus in whom, by the power of the Holy Spirit, all are brought into communion with God (Eph. 1). The church is the foretaste of this communion with God and with one another. The grace of our Lord Jesus Christ, the love of God, and the communion of the Holy Spirit enable the one church to live as sign of the reign of God and servant of the reconciliation with God, promised and provided for the whole creation. The purpose of the church is to unite people with Christ in the power of the Spirit, to manifest communion in prayer and action and thus to point to the fullness of communion with God, humanity and the whole creation in the glory of the Kingdom.[4]

The *ecumenical church* is a manifestation of hope to which I cling! Comprised of a "community of communions" in North America, the ecumenical church seeks to sustain a movement of unity amidst all of the divisions among the churches. The ecumenical church possesses a religious mission and a public role in American society, calling for renewal, rebuilding, and restoring relationships between and among individuals, communities of faith, and those who seek to serve the common good. This movement, based on shared civic and moral principles, is ultimately rooted in the faith that the unity needed to transform every aspect of our life together has already been given by God through Jesus Christ, the One who makes all things possible. The ecumenical movement, therefore, derives its vocation of public witness and advocacy from Christ's mission to transform the whole world and not only the church itself.

As an activist and progressive movement in socially reactionary and economically repressive times, the ecumenical church, through, for example, the programs and services of the National Council of Churches, holds fast to a vision of unity among a broad base of churches and communities which requires nothing less than its total involvement in a variety of public concerns. Because of this mission, the NCCC is often criticized for "sticking its nose in where it doesn't belong." Controversy, however, is no match for the commitment and action of some 150,000 local congregations on whose behalf the Council persistently jumps head-first into stormy waters, often in instances in which churches acting separately have failed to find the common ground needed to bring a crisis to resolution.

The Burned Churches Project is a prime example of the NCCC's aggressive response to the violence and hatred of racism. Far from perfect and not without its detractors, this project typifies the Council's convictions with respect to its religious mission and its public role. However, before moving on to the important work of advocacy and education in racial matters, not least as seen in the Burned Churches Project, we must ask several theological questions of the "ecumenical church."

How are the realities of *koinonia/communio* and *oikumene* to be understood in such concrete circumstances of national crisis as have been experienced during and in the aftermath of the burning of churches? What does *ecumenical solidarity* mean in this context, given the religious and civic implications of the terrorism that has befallen particular worshiping communities and has captured, writ large, the flaws of American society? There are also ecclesiological and ethical issues to be considered in light of the fact that both church and society in America share a vision of "one people" in spite of deep and dividing divisions. How are the basic ecclesiological convictions of the ecumenical church related to public life and to the ethical issues facing society?

In raising such questions, I would commend a text prepared by Philip Potter, former General Secretary of the World Council of Churches (WCC). Although Dr. Potter's words were written for the WCC and thus have a decidedly global concern, there is wisdom in them worth applying to the situation of North American Christians whose convictions and questions about the appropriateness of the church's public role remain persistently unsettling and unclear. Potter writes:

> When we look around us we find a world full of fear and mistrust, of concealment or of exposure in order to destroy rather than to build up, of alienation, of loneliness, of tyranny and powerlessness . . . The whole burden of the ecumenical movement is to cooperate with God in making *oikumene* an *oikos*, a home, a family of men and women, of young and old, of varied gifts, cultures, possibilities, where openness, trust, love and justice reign.[5]

The image of "homemaking" within Dr. Potter's text is striking both in regard to the religious mission of the ecumenical
church and its involvement in the public arena. In its response
to the burning of churches, the NCCC mobilized its resources
in part to help members of "the household," although clearly
the public impact of the Council's witness has extended far beyond its own borders. The burned-out family members included
Baptists, Methodists, Lutherans, Roman Catholics, and Presbyterians, as well as independent community churches. Under
NCCC leadership, the National Conference of Catholic Bishops,
the American Jewish Committee, the Congress of National
Black Churches, the Religious Action Center of Reform Judaism—Union of American Hebrew Congregations, the Islamic
Circle of North America, the Standing Conference of Orthodox
Bishops of America, and the Unitarian Universalist Association,
joined forces in June 1996 to form "the most inclusive ecumenical and interfaith partnership ever developed in our country,"
according to Joan Brown Campbell, NCCC General Secretary.

This inclusive partnership demonstrates that out of this
tragedy it is now possible to glimpse the larger *oikos,* God's
household, at work cooperating as the whole *oikumene* to stand
with and serve family members in need. Equally impressive has
been the support which has come from the public realm, which
has bestowed on the NCCC its trust "to do the right thing" with
donations large and small. No matter how large or how small
those donations of money, time, and skills; no matter the language in which prayers have been lifted; no matter how used
or how new the gifts in kind—choir robes, Bibles, hymnals, pews,
building materials—the ecumenical church, led by the NCCC,
together with its partners of other faiths and the citizens of this
country, placed its religious and civic life on the line, (1) to stand
with the victims of racially motivated hate crimes, (2) to share
in their distress and in the joy of their determination to rebuild
and restore, and (3) to serve both its religious calling to further
the reconciliation "promised and provided for the whole creation"
by God and its vocation of public witness and advocacy as an
expression both of its civic duty and as a sign of the reign of God.

Surely the scourge of racism which preys on innocent persons for no reason other than their race or the color of their

skin, whether cloaked behind the white hoods of extremists or fully exposed in the light of the day in the despicable effects of personal bigotry and institutional discrimination, must be taken as seriously as evil in any form. The evils with which the churches contend are real, but they have not defeated the churches in spite of the wounds on Christ's body. Christian tradition teaches that the only legitimate response to evil is to act non-violently against it, to resist its seductive power. Consequently, retreat is not an option for the church if the evil reign of racism is ever to end and the doers of evil brought to their knees.

The ecumenical church, quite possibly the church in its most authentic and inclusive form this side of the *eschaton*, has both the reason and the resources to confront racism head-on. But does it have the courage to sustain the struggle to its completion? Does it dare test its fragile unity on such issues as the burning of black churches or on a confessional understanding of racism as sin? Such questions are deeply disturbing since there are no apparent or easy answers. Yet, like the phoenix rising from the ashes of its own fiery consumption, the ecumenical church may well rise from the ashes left by the burned black churches in, echoing Baldwin, the fire this time. Perhaps the ecumenical church, self-defined as a community of communions, can be revived by this virulent racism which is causing it faithfully to stand as the servant of God, as an advocate for God's justice on behalf of the victimized. The unselfish and tireless acts of churches and others—at local, regional, and national levels—brought together under the ecclesial and moral shadow of the National Council of Churches specifically to redress the burning of African American churches have sent a clarion call to this nation which has for too long been apathetic, brutally indifferent, and blatantly wrong-headed in race matters.

"Sharing the Fire"

In most rural African communities, kitchens are not equipped with elaborate ranges. Instead, cooking is done over charcoal or wood fires. To start the fire, a young boy or girl may go from house to house to borrow a few burning coals from a neighbor's fireplace. After one's fire starts burning, others arrive to borrow a few burning coals; and so the process of sharing the fire continues. In Scripture, fire is associated with the Holy Spirit. Yet it is also true that "faith comes from what is heard, and what is heard comes through the word of Christ" (Rom. 10:17).[6]

To be sure, our African brothers and sisters are speaking of "sharing the fire" in ways very different from those we have been discussing. Isaac Fokuo is writing about sharing the fire of evangelism and church growth in Africa. What he subsequently offers in the way of a very powerful reflection is qualified by his disclaimer, "this essay is not an attempt to write a theology of evangelism from an African perspective, but rather simply to tell the story as I know it . . . as a Ghanaian whose experience of 'sharing the fire' is limited to my context . . ."[7]

The context of this image, as used by Fokuo, is very specific, "limited." Yet the capacity of this image to transcend its particularity and carry meaning beyond its context to our own is far from limited, precisely because the church's mission to share the fire of God's passion to transform the world through love and justice goes hand in hand with the church's vocation of public witness and advocacy. In the end, sharing the fire this time is a call to action for people of faith and for all others, people who can no longer sit quietly as the power of racism to destroy the fabric of our corporate life as a society is denied, disputed, or once again deployed to foil the credibility and integrity of the ecclesial and civic role of the ecumenical church. Acting in solidarity through the NCCC to protect "visible unity in one faith," as the constitution of the World Council of Churches puts it, churches in America have circled the wagons around burned-out African American churches with prayer, support, and the assistance needed to rebuild. Herein the image, sharing the fire, supplied by our African sisters and brothers transcends its specificity and limitations "for just such a time as this" (Esth. 4:14).

Has the light generated by the dastardly burning of African American churches *ironically* focused on lessons from our tortuous and racially divided history so that to ignore it would be tantamount to rejecting the revelation of Jesus Christ as the light which "shines in the darkness and the darkness did not overcome it" (John 1:5)? This provocative question is genuinely at the heart of this writer's reflection on the legitimacy of the church's ecclesial and public role as an advocate in race matters, its calling to be "the repairer of the breach, the restorer of streets to live in" (Is. 58:12b). It is naive and irresponsible to disregard the legacy of racism as one of the most formidable stumbling blocks to the vision and quest for unity as shared by both church and society. It would also be an act of unforgivable infidelity to the mission and ministry of Jesus Christ not to contend with racism as one of the many fault lines along which his body is strained and broken in the American churches.

I am clear that in race matters, the mission and vocation of advocacy and education undertaken by the ecumenical church, and particularly the NCCC, is integral to the life and mission of the whole body of Christ in the world. Fidelity to the prophetic and gospel traditions requires nothing less than that the churches participate and accept this mission in fulfillment of "their common calling to the glory of the one God" (WCC constitution).

The American context is exacting. I don't begin to understand how to address the need for advocacy and education in the realm of social injustice, whatever the particular issue, without attempting to get at root causes. I don't begin to tolerate the thought that it is either safe or prudent to ignore racist "acts by small groups of sociopaths in different contexts" any more than I think it wise summarily to dismiss the idea that there might somewhere in our land be an agreement or conspiracy, formal or informal, to burn African American churches. The vocation of public witness and advocacy is far too costly an act of solidarity with the victims of evil to be lightly regarded as merely a dramatic and emotional reaction to a series of untoward events. In her March 19, 1997 testimony to the Committee on the Judiciary of the United States House of Representatives, Joan Brown Campbell left little to the imagination concerning the relationship between advocacy, education, and racism:

> . . . our determination is that the fires will end because racism will be tenaciously challenged and hounded out from among us. The conditions of life that are fed by it—poverty, joblessness, inadequate health care, insufficient provisions

for children, educational needs—require our concerted address. The forces that feed it—bigotry, prejudice, hatred, violence, religious narrowness, exclusive social patterns and the like—will require change.

By *sharing the fire* maybe one day racism will no longer divide and terrorize the body of Christ. Racism is sin against God and humanity, for which the church and society must atone together by acknowledging its reality and working to combat it in every form. The ecumenical church's vocation of public witness and advocacy is grounded in movements of social change and transformation, movements rooted in the reign of God. As we pursue our ministries of public witness and advocacy, committed to sharing light from *the fire this time* in hopes of making this *oikos* a safer household for every person, we, like our African brothers and sisters, may come to realize that this time "the fire is now our fire." The question is, what will we dare do with it?

I am indebted to the Rev. Isaac Fokuo, a pastor in the Presbyterian Church of Ghana, for the title of this essay. I hope that by this choice of title Pastor Fokuo's concern for the "African church to take its ideas, its faith, and its fire to the world" has been honored and respected in some small way.

Notes

1. James Baldwin, *The Fire Next Time* (New York: The Dial Press, 1963), pp. 119–20.
2. *Ebony,* September 1996.
3. Ibid.
4. A statement prepared by the Commission on Faith and Order and adopted by the World Council of Churches at its 7th Assembly, Canberra, Australia, 1992.
5. *The Ecumenical Review,* 1977.
6. Isaac K. Fokuo, in *The Journey Continues,* 1995.
7. Ibid.

9

The Ecumenical Movement and Racism

Susan E. Davies

The eruption of destruction which we have seen in the last two and one-half years is a portent of the rotting timbers at the foundation of white American society and its churches. The burning, bombing, and vandalism perpetrated against houses of worship across the country are violent signs of structural evil which will, if left unattended, destroy the churches of the United States. For white Christians in America, the sign of a seven-year-old white child attacking a rural black church must cause us to confess the wickedness we have created and too often silently continue to condone: the racist structures upon which we have built this nation and our churches. White Christians must acknowledge the depth of the racism which infects our churches, and work to eradicate this apostasy which makes a mockery of our claim to be the body of Christ.

Many white Christians, along with their black, Hispanic, Asian, and Native American brothers and sisters, have in fact been working with increasing urgency and insight to extirpate this evil. The World and National Councils of Churches, as well as Faith and Order, have worked for generations to identify and undo the racism which has infected churches and communities engaged in ecumenical dialogue. This paper will begin with an analysis of the nature of racism, present a theological imperative for undoing this Christian apostasy, delineate some of the history of Faith and Order in its anti-racism work, and offer alternative perspectives from which to live faithfully. The work of undoing racism, while many generations old, will be the churches' responsibility into the future. The demands of the gospel and the smoke from burning churches require nothing less.

The Nature of Racism

Racism begins with the belief that races actually exist and that they divide the one human family into a variety of racial groupings. Such a belief is non-biblical. The Western version of it is the outgrowth of religious intolerance dating back at least to the Middle Ages in Europe. Whereas the Bible speaks of tribes, kindreds, tongues, nations, and peoples to describe different groups of human beings, the only references to race in the biblical text are to contests such as foot races.[1] According to Rena Karefa-Smart, "Until it is understood that . . . a deeply rooted notion of 'race' is unwarranted scientifically and *theologically*, population groups will continue to be identified in ways that reify what does not exist . . ."[2]

Once the belief in different human races has been established, racism can begin to develop its deadly hold. Racism is neither bigotry nor prejudice. To be prejudiced is to "have opinions without knowing the facts and to hold onto those opinions, even after contrary facts are known. To be racially prejudiced means to have distorted opinions about people of other races."[3] Everyone in every ethnic group has prejudices about those within and outside their own group. It is not possible to grow up in the United States, or in any other nation, without being racially prejudiced, no matter to which "race" one has been assigned by birth or custom. Racial prejudice only becomes racism "when one racial group becomes so powerful and dominant that it is able to control another group and to enforce the controlling group's biases."[4]

Joseph Barndt offers an excellent brief summary of the nature of racism in *Dismantling Racism: The Continuing Challenge to White America.* He, along with most others who work in this field, defines racism as *prejudice plus power*. He is clear that the central issue in racism is the use of economic, social, religious, and political power by one group to control the lives of others.

> Racism (prejudice plus power) develops when personal opinion and individual bigotry are codified and enforced as societal behavior. Racism structures a society so that the prejudices of one racial group are taught, perpetuated and

enforced to the benefit of the dominant group. Racism harnesses the energies and loyalties of the dominant group for that group's purposes. Racism provides better services and facilities for the dominant group through that group's institutions. Racism decrees more severe restrictions and control over its victims than it does over the dominant group.[5]

Christian racism can be most easily recognized in the United States from the existence of the historic black churches and the predominantly white churches. It is evident more covertly in the hymnals of the white denominations prior to the 1990s, in the pictures of Jesus which hang in the smallest Sunday school room in northern Maine, in selective images used in sermons every Sunday across the land, in biblical geography which separates Egypt from Africa, to say nothing of the direct preaching of racial hatred and suspicion in white supremacist groups which carry the cross. Mainline white churches within the United States have historically made specific decisions which demonstrate how racism has defined and infiltrated the body. I cite only three such cases from Barndt:

> It was, for example, a deliberate and historically traceable decision within some denominations to give their boards of "foreign missions" the assignment to do evangelism among people of color in the United States. It was a deliberate and historically traceable decision in some denominations to develop separate seminaries for people of color. . . . Thousands of congregations from almost every denomination followed their constituencies from the cities to the suburbs because of the influx of people of color.[6]

Theological Principles Opposing Racism

Racism takes many shapes in our culture and in our churches. It is a sin and an apostasy because it violates the very core of our rebirth at baptism. Christians of every time and culture, every economic and social context, every language and every color, are one body in Christ. We are neither Jew nor Greek, male nor female, slave nor free. When we conceive of ourselves as divided by racial identity, we violate the new identity we are given in our baptism. When we allow racial division to deform our relationships within the church, we violate the body of Christ. In Deborah Mullen's words,

> . . . the problem of racism in the Church is an issue of Christian "family values." . . . If baptism is the basis of our unity in all matters concerning the faith we hold in common, is not racist belief and practice among baptized Christians a scandal within the fellowship of believers? Is it not also a blind spot on the Church's vision of visible unity and an obvious obstacle to living out our discipleship more faithfully in accordance with our one baptism into one faith and one common life in Christ? . . . Racism within the Christian family is one more grisly manifestation of the fragmentation of the body of Christ . . . [and] . . . is tearing the family of God apart . . ."[7]

The burning and bombed churches of the United States stand as witness to the depth of Christian racism. The perpetrators may be motivated by a variety of causes, from personal gain to revenge to outright racial and religious hatred, but underlying all individual decisions, all the plans of each small group which engages in the attacks is the conviction, spread by white Christians, that races exist, and that God prefers some over others, that God prefers one particular creed, one particular eucharistic witness, one particular skin color or language or economic stratum over all others.

Christian identity and community are rooted and grounded in Christ. "At the center is trust in God's love in Christ, and at the ever-changing edges is the practice of hospitality and service."[8] Christians are embodied, enculturated beings who are part of the dominion of God. We are not generic beings; we come in different ages, shapes, colors, and dispositions. We are Republican and Democrat and Greens, European and African, Timorese, Bulgarian, Andean, Mongolian and American, Orthodox and Pentecostal, feminist and fundamental, newly reborn and ancient in our tradition. We are part of one race, the human race, and live in many historical and cultural settings. We are each peculiar to our time and place, and we are part of a body which stretches back more than two thousand years as well as forward into a future still being born of God. We are connected to one another because we are part of the same race of beings, and because, as Christians, we are part of the same body of Christ.

Ecumenical Anti-Racism Work

Central to any orthodox conception of the church is the fundamental conviction that racism is incompatible with faith in the Triune God. According to Jeffrey Gros, "until the stigma of racism is eradicated from the Church, it cannot be a credible witness to the Apostolic Faith or to the one, holy, catholic and apostolic Church it is called to be in Christ."[9]

During the twentieth century, the ecumenical movement has developed a growing awareness of the theological nature of racism as a church dividing reality. While African American churches were represented from the very beginning of Faith and Order in 1927 and of the World Council of Churches in 1948, the existence of racially defined separations within the body of Christ was for decades merely noted as one of the differences dividing the churches. In 1952 at the Third World Conference on Faith and Order held at Lund, Sweden, the issues of "social, contextual and institutional barriers to church union" was removed from the category of "non-theological factors" and recognized as equivalent in importance to faith, order, and worship as issues which divide the church.[10] Such "relevant social, cultural, political, racial and other factors" are embedded in the constitution of Faith and Order as matters which bear fundamentally on the unity of the church. The 1993 Fifth World Conference on Faith and Order, Santiago de Compostella, Spain, once again declared in its message to the churches that "only a church that overcomes ethnic, racial and national hatreds in a common Christian and human identity can be a credible sign of freedom and reconciliation."[11]

For the past eighty years, the ecumenical movement has struggled with the causes and consequences of racism in the church. Rena Karefa-Smart has identified three stages in that struggle: the period of "resolutionary" anti-racism work, the "struggle for social justice," and the current era in which we seek to move beyond Christian racism.[12]

During the first half of this century, ecumenical groups and councils of churches addressed the problem of "race relations" by praising diversity and deploring the tensions between various racial groups. Resolutions regularly attacked racial injustice and urged racial equality. The second period, roughly from 1965 to 1985, was one in which increasing attention was given to the complex social, economic, and political realities which both produced and continue to support the oppressive conditions relative to the spread of European colonialism. During this period the Program to Combat Racism was created by the World Council of Churches. The Program funded a variety of educational and political actions designed to create new models of solidarity and witness, and labored against white supremacy and white racism.

Karefa-Smart sees the present and future as a time of uncovering the false nature of race as a biological and theological reality as we move toward a non-racial world:

> The problem is not that racism is simply a "fringe" aspect of Christianity, one embraced by those who have not grasped the core of the gospel—though such people and groups certainly are dramatic in their racism—for that would be a fairly easy thing to disavow and root out. Rather the racism about which we are concerned here is like the worm in the core of the apple: quietly, with no fanfare and little external sign, it has made itself at home, and the rot has spread at the very heart of Christian communities.[13]

During the last two decades, Faith and Order in the United States has attended carefully to the theological and ecclesiological implications of racism as a church-dividing issue. Its ecumenical membership has been reminded again and again that, in the words of Gayraud Wilmore and David Shannon,

> too many theological discussions and studies neglect the fact that we are not called to love in word and in speech, but in deed and in truth (1 John 3:18). No amount of profound theologizing about the necessity of the Nicene Creed or the coherence of Baptism, Eucharist and Ministry will please God nearly as much as loosening the bonds of wickedness

in the church, letting the oppressed go free, and breaking every yoke (Is. 58:6).[14]

Beginning in 1990, the Working Group on Unity and Renewal of Faith and Order, which had previously addressed the church-dividing nature of the AIDS epidemic, turned its attention to white racism as a church-dividing issue. The product of our work, as already indicated in this essay, is forthcoming under the working title, *Ending Racism in the Church,* and much of the work cited here is from that book. During the long struggle to determine both the nature and the structure of our work, we learned with and from one another the painful realities of racism as both a church-dividing and painful interpersonal issue.

As one of the European Americans in the group, I can testify to the fear and reluctance which occupied many of the white members: will I sound like a bigot? will I be the focus of scorn and rejection because of my ignorance and unacknowledged racism? At the same time some of the African Americans in the group were reluctant to commit themselves to yet one more effort to educate white folks, perhaps especially well-meaning theological types. The very nature of white racism means that addressing the issue seems to be an option for European Americans, while African Americans cannot escape the detrimental effects of the apostasy. We labored together over six years to produce our book, and the white people among us learned more deeply and fully how fundamental is the division caused by racism in the body of Christ.

The Burned Churches

The immediate occasion for this book, *Out of the Ashes,* is the burning, bombing, and vandalism of houses of worship in the United States over the past few years. The National Church Arson Task Force has investigated "369 arsons, bombings or attempted bombings that have occurred at houses of worship between January 1, 1995 and March 12, 1997."[15] The houses of worship which have been attacked include synagogues and Muslim temples as well as churches. Among the churches, buildings occupied by African Americans both Muslim and

Christian, white Christians and inter-ethnic Christians have all been attacked. Of the 369 houses of worship attacked by bombing, attempted bombings, or arson throughout the United States through March 12, 1997, 155 have been African American. Among the churches attacked in the South, 53.3% or 105 have been black churches; most of those buildings belonged to rural, poor congregations.[16]

Of the total number of arrests (175 as of March 12, 1997) for these attacks, in connection with 126 fires at churches and other houses of worship, 73.4% were white males; 66.7% of those arrested for attacking African American houses of worship have been white. African American males have accounted for 16.1% of the arrests at all houses of worship and 31.5% of African American houses of worship. In one case, the pastor of the church has been convicted of the attack. While racial bigotry and religious hatred have been predominant factors in the attacks, other reasons have included financial profit, personal revenge, vandalism, and the simple desire to "burn down a symbol of authority in the community."[17]

Most distressing to this reader of the reports is the fact that 43.2% of those arrested thus far (62: 56 male, 6 female) have been *under 18* and 17.5% have been between the ages of 7 and 13 (25: 22 male, 3 female). Random or targeted acts of violence against houses of worship have been perpetrated by seven year olds!

Attacks on any houses of worship are attacks on all of us, because we are all bound to one another. Christians are bound to Christians by the simple act of baptism into the body of Christ. All human beings are bound to one another by the simple reality of our common humanity. But, as Delores Williams notes, an attack on a black church building is an attack on the heart of the black community.[18]

The black church has nurtured identity and resistance, schools and businesses, political careers and literary, musical and artistic genius for generations of African Americans. But most importantly, says Williams, the black church has been "the creator of community, the sustainer of hope, the liberator redeeming the Black spirit from all that would destroy it." Attacks on the buildings created by black congregations are attacks on "the sacredness of both human and divine Spirit. For Black Americans, these assaults on our churches are no less than attacks on the very spirit of our people."[19]

And these assaults grow out of the racism which has been created and supported by much of the theology and ecclesiology of the Western church for the last two thousand years. The attacks find their immediate and fertile soil in the social, economic, and political conditions prevalent in the United States in the late twentieth century. But they are undergirded by centuries and generations of teaching and practice which have divided the body of Christ every bit as seriously as have our liturgical and creedal formulations. We are held accountable in the sight of God for supporting and repeating the lies of racial oppression and bigotry in our preaching, in our homes, and at our divided eucharistic table.

Overcoming Christian Racism

Christian racism always manifests itself most clearly in the other person rather than within ourselves. It was easy for most white North Americans to understand the evil of apartheid and the sinful nature of the theology which undergirded it. It was easy for northern white Christians to see the evil of southern segregation and the wickedness of the theology which justified slavery. It is much more difficult for white North American Christians to look in the mirror and see themselves as merely one of the many different types of people created by God in the human race, rather than as the normative white race by which all other Christians, to say nothing of other humans, are to be evaluated. It is much easier to invite "others" into "our" worship, expecting them to accommodate to our normative ways, than to be changed ourselves into a new and living community.

Jack Hayford made a similar discovery about his response as an "evangelical" to the liberal white involvement in the civil rights movement of the 1960s. "I'd presumptuously think, 'Oh, that's those liberals, that's all they've got to do. They are not interested in the spread of the Gospel, so they just go down and march with the blacks for the sake of some political issue.'" Only much later did he realize the lack of love he had shown for his "brothers who were totally as evangelical as I was—my black brothers—[who] felt I forsook them by my non-involvement in the civil rights movement."[20] Racism, white Christian racism, takes many forms in many contexts.

I grew up in a racially divided world. My neighborhood in Detroit was white; a nearby wealthier neighborhood supplied nearly all the leaders of our congregation and their neighborhood was marked by a whites-only real estate covenant. I was taught at youth group and church camp to value diversity, to support the rights of those who were "less fortunate" and to give freely from my own bounty to those who were "needy." The language of race was largely couched in *noblesse oblige,* in which it was regarded as the duty of the superior groups to give "not a hand out but a hand up" to those who needed assistance in competing against the better educated and trained native born, English-speaking, northern and western European white people (Poles, Jews, Italians, and Catholics need not apply). The "resolutionary ecumenism" of which Karefa-Smart speaks was well developed in our context, and I imbibed racial distinctions along with my earliest Bible stories.

Our youth group spent parts of several summers helping to rebuild "inner city" buildings used by black (we said "Negro" then) youth groups for their neighborhood support services. We never questioned why they did not come to help us in our work, nor why they needed our help in the first place. We simply knew that we were responsible for assisting our "lesser" brothers and sisters in Christ, lesser because they were Negro and because they were poor.

We sang freedom songs at church camp, and listened to freedom riders tell us of conditions and actions far beyond our ken. We knew, as white northerners, that racism was a problem "they" had. In my high school of 5000 students, there were four blacks, none of whom I knew or remembered until I looked recently at my yearbook. That my life and my church was as segregated as Little Rock, as divided as Selma, simply never entered my mind.

During my senior year in high school I travelled with other white youth from Michigan on a "Southern Tour" of colleges and schools founded by the American Missionary Association during and after the Civil War. We stayed in the dorms at Fisk and Tuskegee, worshiped with our hosts in black rural and urban churches, and were grateful for the medical assistance at Taladega when one of our group needed dental care. That care was given by the first black dentist any of us had encountered.

It was a trip into another world, with different perspectives, different social organizations, and different ways of understanding what I had always seen as normative white culture. The intellectual and theological equipment I had at the time for understanding that trip was what Karefa-Smart has called "resolutionary" anti-racism. I agreed with strong positions on racial equality, was angry about racial injustice, and wrote a stinging paper for my senior English class on whites-only residential covenants. (My teacher assured me that my idealism would be tempered as I matured.)

I was, however, blind to the interweavings of social, economic, and political structures with the theological stance of my church. I could pray about being washed whiter than snow without a twinge, use language inside and outside worship which valued whiteness over darkness without seeing the underlying assumptions, and learn about the Ethiopian eunuch without knowing the generations who had suffered because that story was used to justify the inferiority of all Africans to all Europeans. When I heard about the "Black Jesus" at the church in Detroit led by my brother in the United Church of Christ, Al Cleague, I was as puzzled then by a black Jesus as many men are today about the need for female language for God.

When the Program to Combat Racism began at the World Council of Churches, I supported it. I agreed that the Reformation affirmation of the right of resistance against tyranny was equally the right of people of color around the globe. What I have come to see more clearly in the intervening years is how thoroughly and completely racism is embedded in the very structures of Christian thought as developed in the white West over the last two thousand years.

The Marks of the Church

Several years ago, Letty Russell proposed a revision of the marks of the church which has direct relevance to the work at hand in this book. She began by reminding us all that the church has "no nature of its own because its existence is derived from Christ's presence."[21] She then proceeded to look at the historical marks of the church: unity, holiness, catholicity, and apostolicity, and observed that the "understanding of church shifts when we interpret [those marks] . . . from the point of view of those at the periphery of life, society and the church."[22] Her argument is clear: "The signs themselves cannot make the presence of Christ clear if they do not show that presence forth among the poor and as signs of a mended creation, as well as in the witness, liturgy and gathering of the community."[23]

The subject of this book, *Out of the Ashes*, the burning of houses of worship throughout the United States, requires that we face the divisions in our midst and look at them from an unfamiliar angle, one which will allow us to see the effects of racism as a church-dividing reality. Much of the work of the ecumenical movement over the last century has addressed means by which various churches could recognize in one another's creedal, organizational, and sacramental lives the marks of the church. In the face of the rising tide of hatred, the growing numbers of white supremacist groups in the United States, and the painful public refusal of many political leaders any longer to stand against both the causes and the effects of white racism in this country, it is time for the churches to look seriously at the divisive power of the racial divide which continues to deepen within and among us.

Letty Russell argues that the *unity* of the church can best be discerned in those places where the church is breaking down barriers, "at points where people are being excluded," rather than merely by agreement on creeds or ordination. The *holiness* of the church, she says, can be tested by "how well it announces justice and denounces forces that hinder the appearance of God's righteousness in the mending of creation." *Catholicity*, similarly, can be seen in "how well the church lives out the sign of Christ's universal presence in the world . . . [through] the quality of connectedness in solidarity with those on the periphery of church and society." And *apostolicity* is seen most clearly in the church's "constancy in participation in God's Mission" to embody hope and justice for the whole of God's created world.[24]

The Burned Churches Project of the National Council of the Churches of Christ in the USA is an ecumenical testimony to the reality of these marks of the church. By deeds of solidarity and acts of justice, through participation in God's mission of hope, and by denouncing the racism at the core of these burnings, the National Council has moved to reshape our understanding of the church's unity, holiness, catholicity, and apostolicity. This work, however, will only come to full fruition when it has moved as it has intended: to dismantle the structural and Christian racism which infects both church and society in the United States. In the words of Joan Brown Campbell, "We see in the burnings of these churches the broken body of Christ. We are all one family, related by the blood of Jesus. We are blood relatives. That leaves no room for racism."[25]

For this essay, the author is deeply indebted to colleagues in Faith and Order, whose common labor over the last six years has produced the forthcoming book, *Ending Racism in the Church* (Cleveland: United Church Press, 1998).

Notes

1. Tee Garlington, "The Eucharist and Racism," in *Ending Racism in the Church*, (Cleveland: United Church Press, forthcoming 1998).

2. Rena Karefa-Smart, "Beyond Our Roots: A Call to Move Beyond Christian Racism into a Nonracial Church for a Nonracial World," Ibid.

3. Joseph Barndt, *Dismantling Racism: The Continuing Challenge to White America* (Minneapolis: Augsburg Press, 1991), p. 28.

4. Ibid., p. 29.

5. Ibid.

6. Ibid., p. 146.

7. Deborah Flemister Mullen, "Baptism: Sacrament of Struggle and Rite of Resistance," in *Ending Racism in the Church*, op. cit.

8. Letty M. Russell, *Church in the Round: Feminist Interpretation of the Church* (Louisville: Westminster/John Knox, 1993), p. 159.

9. Jeffrey Gros, FSC, "God's Will and Our Unity: Toward a Sharing of Gifts and Struggles," in *Ending Racism in the Church*, op. cit.

10. Ibid.

11. Cited in Gros, op. cit.

12. Rena Karefa-Smart, op. cit.

13. Ibid.

14. David T. Shannon and Gayraud S. Wilmore, eds., *Black Witness to the Apostolic Faith* (Grand Rapids: Wm. B. Eerdmans Publishing Co., 1988), p. vii.

15. Joint Statement of James E. Johnson, Assistant Secretary (Enforcement) Department of the Treasury and Isabelle Katz Pinzler, Acting Assistant Attorney General, Civil Rights Division, Department of Justice, Co-Chairs, National Church Arson Task Force before the House Judiciary Committee, March 19, 1997, p. 2.

16. Percentages drawn from the Interim Report for the President, National Church Arson Task Force, United States Department of the Treasury, United States Department of Justice, Bureau of Alcohol, Tobacco and Firearms, Federal Bureau of Investigation, January, 1997.

17. Joint Statement, op. cit., p. 13.

18. Delores S. Williams, "Violence Against God," *The Other Side* (September-October, 1996), p. 19.

19. Ibid.

20. Jack W. Hayford, "An Evangelical Response to Racism," An address to the 1995 convention of the National Association of Evangelicals, unpublished manuscript, pp. 12, 14.

21. Letty M. Russell, op. cit., p. 131.

22. Ibid., p. 132.

23. Ibid.

24. Ibid., pp. 133–135.

25. Joan Brown Campbell, "A Letter from Rev. Dr. Joan Brown Campbell," Burned Churches Newsletter, "Out of the Ashes," Vol. 1, No. 1 (New York: National Council of Churches, November 1996), p. 2.

10

A Matter of Faith and Order

William G. Rusch

This collection of essays is based on a thesis that in fact is one of the core presuppositions of the ecumenical movement: theological reflection about the scandal of visible disunity among the churches is an essential ingredient in overcoming that disunity. Indeed, such reflection provides a basis for the churches to act together in mission toward the world. This theological enterprise must be in an integral albeit intricate relation with the churches for the sake of both unity and mission. Theological reflection alone is without result; action alone is without definition and purpose.

The ecumenical movement itself challenges the churches to do their theology together in a way that is ecclesial/ecumenical and which has implications for their common action. If this assertion is true, and practiced even to some degree by the member churches of the National Council of the Churches of Christ in the USA, it provides an explanation of why more than thirty churches that can appear, act, and sound so differently, have banded together to address a major social evil in the United States today, and to offer of their material resources to alleviate the situation.

Admittedly several explanations could be offered, and they might all contain an element of truth. The underlying proposal of this book, however, is that the churches have lived and thought together *in a conciliar context,* in some cases for nearly fifty years, within the National Council of Churches. This experience has altered their sense of Christian identity and Christian responsibility. There is thus a theological, not merely a social reason for their common action. The existence of *Out of the Ashes* demonstrates this contention although it has not always been a matter of conscious awareness.

This common action, motivated by ecclesial/ecumenical theologizing, pushes the churches inevitably to a series of questions for which at the present time there are no easy or obvious answers. What difference does it make that churches reflect and act together in responding to ethical decisions? What difference does this experience of the churches make in the way the nature of the church is understood? Is there some kind of an ecclesial dimension in the reality of Christians coming together across confessional and traditional lines and in attempting to be "Christ for others"? Finally, and perhaps most sharply: If churches are not engaging in the issues of the contemporary scene, are they being fully church? As in this instance, when churches in the ecumenical movement grapple with urgent social issues, they are not reducing the need for ecclesial/ecumenical theology; rather, they are making such theology all the more imperative.

Contrary to some opinions, it is not strange that both the present reflection and action are occurring within the context of the ecumenical movement. That movement is the search for visible unity in the truth found in Jesus Christ and into which the Holy Spirit leads. It is a quest for the gift of the Triune God, for the visible unity of God's people. If that statement seems paradoxical, it should! Yet this ecumenical movement is, and always has been, multidimensional, a search for the will of God in all areas of life and work. It is neither the building of the Kingdom, nor is it a quietism unmoved by the world's needs. Justice, peace, cultural, and ethical issues all fall within the purview of the ecumenical movement. It is not always tidy. Different agendas have competed with each other. Painfully it has been learned that not every issue can be addressed simultaneously. Much of the present tension within the ecumenical movement involves the struggle to preserve the integrity and essential indivisibility of the movement and to retain the various items that belong within the movement, including social and ethical concerns.

The answer to this tension, or perhaps answers, has not been easy to come upon in the ecumenical movement. But surely the final answer, whatever its specific language, must bear a form that begins with the visible unity of the church as a "fully reconciled communion/fellowship" that leads from the one common baptism and the one common confession of Christ, from fellowship at the altar, and from common prayer, to a common service for sisters and brothers, and on to common action directed toward the world. To state the matter in this way, it must be pointed out, is by no means to imply that common action in this world must await a fully reconciled communion.

In this context it is most natural and necessary that the Faith and Order movement within the one ecumenical movement should encourage theological reflection such as appears in this volume. This follows from the nature of Faith and Order. For that movement serves the churches by leading them into theological dialogue in order to overcome obstacles and to discover new ways to the unity that the Lord of the church wills. Its aim is to proclaim the oneness of the church of Jesus Christ and to call the churches to the goal of visible unity in one faith and one eucharistic fellowship, expressed in worship and in common life in Christ "in order that the world may believe" (cf. John 17). But on the way to this goal, Faith and Order has been aware that the churches are called to become a believable sign and instrument of God's intention for the salvation and transformation of all humanity and all creation.

On the world level, Faith and Order has pursued such studies as "The Church as Mystery and Prophetic Sign" and "The Unity of the Church and Renewal of Human Community," the latter published as *Church and World* (Geneva: WCC Publications, Faith and Order Paper No. 151, 1990). As early as its meetings in Lund in 1952, Montreal in 1963, Canterbury in 1969, and Louvain in 1971, the Commission on Faith and Order of the World Council of Churches took up the issue of racism. At Accra in 1974 the Commission took formal action to collaborate with the WCC Program to Combat Racism, to contribute to this program on the theological level, and to learn better from this experience to face the problem of racism as an issue of church unity. In 1976 the Commission produced a study, "Racism in Theology—Theology Against Racism." Moreover, at the most recent world conference on Faith and Order in Santiago de Compostella, Spain, in 1993, Archbishop Desmond Tutu of South Africa delivered a major address on racism as an issue for Faith and Order.

The present World Council of Churches study on ecclesiology and ethics—involving Unit I, which includes the Faith and

Order tradition, and Unit III, which includes the Life and Work tradition—discloses the commitment of Faith and Order to address social and ethical questions that have a church-dividing character. Without entering here into an evaluation of such documents as *Costly Unity, Costly Commitment,* and *Costly Obedience* (cf. Thomas F. Best and Martin Robra, eds., *Ecclesiology and Ethics* [Geneva: World Council of Churches, 1997]), or the motif of "reflection and action," it can be stated that the existence of such texts reveals the desire of ecumenists to find an adequate relation between the discussions about visible unity and ethical concerns. If the exact description of that relationship has proven elusive, the recognition of the legitimacy of the problem has not.

Such efforts have had their parallels in the United States. The historic African American churches have participated in the National Council of Churches' Commission on Faith and Order since its beginnings. In the late 1980s a consultation on "Unity and Renewal / Black Churches in the USA" was designed to encourage a dialogue between Faith and Order of the World Council of Churches and the black churches of the U.S. and to reflect the unique experience and insight of these churches. In the same decade Faith and Order published its study, *Black Witness to the Apostolic Faith,* edited by David T. Shannon and Gayraud Wilmore (Grand Rapids: Wm. B. Eerdmans, 1985). In 1991 a study group of the U.S. Commission completed its final report, "Racism as a Church Uniting /Church Dividing Issue." It is anticipated that another such Faith and Order study on racism is to appear in 1998.

Thus the concern of Faith and Order within the ecumenical movement, including the Commission on Faith and Order of the National Council of Churches, to consider theologically the issue of racism and to call the churches to engage as churches *and* ecumenically with this subject is nothing new. And so it is that *Out of the Ashes: Burned Churches and the Community of Faith* has its place in a long tradition of Faith and Order's proper work. Yet in another sense, *Out of the Ashes* is new. It is a fresh indication with a wider significance of the intention of Faith and Order to reflect theologically on a legitimate and crucial problem, a sin, that churches committed to the ecumenical movement must not avoid. Racism.

If these essays in even some small measure accomplish this task of reflection, then it will become obvious that Faith and Order is still about its historic mandate "to proclaim the oneness of the Church of Jesus Christ and to call the churches to the goal of visible unity in one faith and one eucharistic fellowship in worship and in common life in order that the world may believe."

Contributors

Herb Boyd, New York City, is Media Consultant to the Burned Churches Project and a free-lance journalist.

Joan Brown Campbell, New York City, is General Secretary of the National Council of the Churches of Christ in the USA.

Emmanuel Clapsis, Westwood, Massachusetts, is a priest, theologian, and ecumenist of the Greek Orthodox Archdiocese of America.

Susan E. Davies, Bangor, Maine, is Academic Dean and Jonathan Fisher Professor of Christian Education at the Bangor Theological Seminary.

James H. Evans, Jr., Rochester, New York, is President and Robert K. Davies Professor of Systematic Theology at Colgate Rochester Divinity School, Bexley Hall, Crozer Theological Seminary.

Norman A. Hjelm, Wynnewood, Pennsylvania, is a former Director of the Commission on Faith and Order, National Council of Churches.

Jesse L. Jackson, Sr., Washington, D.C., is President of the Rainbow/PUSH Coalition.

Deborah Flemister Mullen, Chicago, Illinois, is Assistant Professor of Ministry and Historical Studies and Associate Dean at the McCormick Theological Seminary.

Albert M. Pennybacker, New York City, is Associate General Secretary for Public Policy of the National Council of Churches and President of the Ecumenical Development Initiative.

Donald Rojas, New York City, is Director of the Burned Churches Project.

William G. Rusch, New York City, is Director of the Commission on Faith and Order, National Council of Churches.

Melvin G. Talbert, West Sacramento, California, is Bishop of the United Methodist Church, San Francisco Area, and President of the National Council of Churches, 1996–97.

Philip Turner, New Haven, Connecticut, is Dean of the Berkeley Divinity School at Yale University.

McKinley Young, Atlanta, Georgia, is Bishop of the African Methodist Episcopal Church, Office of Ecumenical and Urban Affairs.